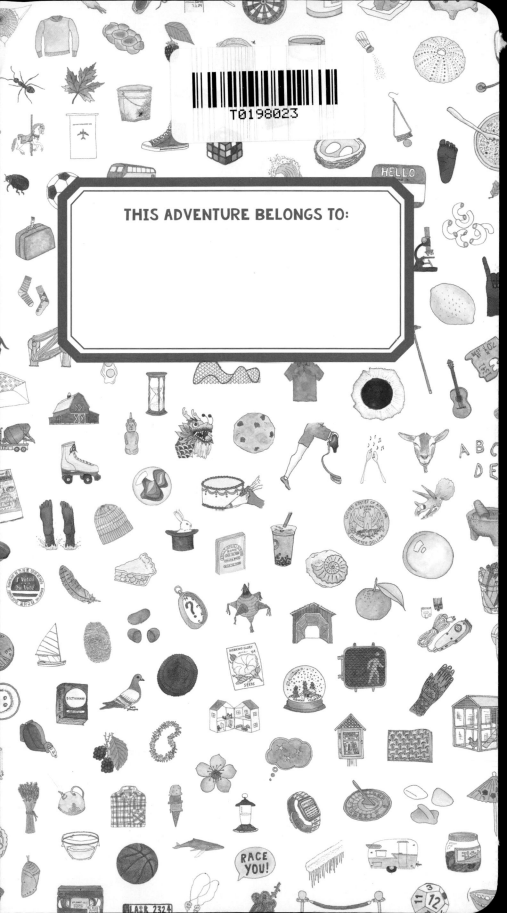

THIS ADVENTURE BELONGS TO:

HELLO

T0198023

RACE YOU!

WONDER HUNT

A SEEK-AND-FIND BINGO ADVENTURE

By
LEA REDMOND

WONDER HUNT

I am delighted to have you join me on this adventure!

A wonder is something—an object, a place, a creature, a sound—that prompts us to think "Wow!" Moments of wonder can be surprising, mysterious, and astonishing. They make us think, laugh, and even cry. Sometimes wonder is obvious and loud, like a lightning storm. Other times it is subtle and quiet. We must pay close attention to notice the elegance of a snail trail glistening on the sidewalk.

Wonder is a noun and an adjective: *a wonder, wonderful.* It is also a verb, something we do: *to wonder.* The ordinary can become extraordinary if we approach it with an open, curious mind and heart. When we do, the world—the people, plants, animals, and artifacts—shows us how wonderful it is.

NICE TO MEET YOU!

HI!

Please call me Aunt Lea. I am an explorer of the everyday. I am also an artist, writer, and teacup collector. For me, looking for wonders is a way of loving the world. Finding a wonder also means that the world loves me back. When I find something good, I feel grateful. Wonder is my friend, my teacher, and my daily companion. But it is only there for me if I am also there for it. *Um, what exactly does that mean, Aunt Lea?* It means that everyday wonder only comes out to play if we are present for it—if we observe carefully, ask good questions, and take time to enjoy whatever we find.

HUNT, PLAY, AND TRACK

This book is a treasure hunt, a bingo game, and a field journal. You are holding an epic list of 500 wonders! They are sorted into 20 different chapters, but you can search for the wonders in any order. As you find a wonder, mark it on its bingo board as "found" with a bingo chip sticker. You can play for "Bingo!" (5 in a row: horizontally, vertically, or diagonally) or challenge yourself for "Blackout!" (all 25 on a board). Each time you find a wonder, you'll take time to observe it and then document it in its section of the field journal. *I've never heard of some of these wonders, Aunt Lea.* Research is part of the game! Ask a friend, family member, or the internet. Visit a library, museum, or store.

HOW TO PLAY

1) Pay attention.

Notice what is around you at all times. Explore with all of your senses and keep an open mind and heart. Remember, wonders are everywhere! Some are easy to find, others can take a long time to locate. For these more rare wonders, think about where you might find them and actively seek them out. Whether you find what you were looking for or not, you will surely experience good things.

2) You decide what counts.

Along the way, you control how much to challenge yourself. Seek a "tight" match that is very close to the one I suggest, or a "looser" match. It's up to you.

For example, wonder #6 is "mitten." It is absolutely okay if your "mitten" is yellow or polka-dotted instead of looking like mine. *But, gosh, Aunt Lea, what if I find a glove?* You decide! If you think a glove is close enough to a mitten, that's fine by me. It's also okay if you want to keep searching for a mitten, or even one just like mine.

If a wonder is too far away or difficult to access, get creative! If you live someplace where it never snows, perhaps your "snowball" can be a snow cone. Can't visit fireflies in person? Find some in a book or movie.

For the "wild" item on each board, you choose! *Anything, Aunt Lea?* Well, I challenge you to find a wonder that fits into that board's theme. Otherwise, yes, anything you want!

3) Celebrate with a sticker.

Find a wonder, earn a bingo chip! Take one sticker from the sheets in the front pocket and place it in that chapter's bingo board on top of the wonder you found. But don't stop here! The best is yet to come . . .

PLACE YOUR BINGO CHIP ON THE WONDER YOU FIND! ⟶

4) Linger a little longer.

I love to hang out with a wonder after I find one, just to see what happens. *But Aunt Lea, what if it's not doing anything.* It is! Get closer and notice details. Get curious about the wonder's story—its past, present, and future. I try to assume that everything is interesting. I just need to figure out how.

MITTEN

Date: 3 /17 22   6

Location: Library Steps

☐ Plain   ☒ Patterned   ☐ On hand

I wonder:

How does this material help keep my hands so warm?!

5) *Log each wonder.*

❋ You will "collect" each wonder by logging it into this field journal. There's no need to physically take the wonders with you. The goal is to seek, find, and experience.

❋ Find your wonder's field journal spot. Log the wonder by drawing it or writing about it, or both! Document any details that make the wonder special.

❋ Circle or check off any of the three descriptors that are true for the particular specimen you have found. Choose none, some, or add your own.

❋ Compose a curiosity for your wonder and enter it at the "I wonder:" prompt. **What's a curiosity, Aunt Lea?** It's a question, an observation, or reflection. Your curiosity might be about how something works, where it came from, or you might want to celebrate an aspect of the wonder that made you laugh. I've shared three curiosities with you at the beginning of each chapter.

Here are a few more curiosities:

WHERE DOES THE WATER IN MY KITCHEN SINK COME FROM?

• • •

A BEAUTIFUL PATTERN IS HIDING IN THE CROSS SECTION OF A CARROT!

• • •

WHAT IS THE TALLEST CAKE THAT HAS EVER BEEN BAKED? HOW MANY LAYERS DID IT HAVE?

PLAY SOLO OR PLAY SOCIALLY!

Feel free to play alone or in groups, or even mix and match these methods for different chapters.

* **COOPERATE.** *Version A:* Work together by sharing one book and passing it back and forth. You can mail it to a faraway teammate. *Version B:* Two or more players can seek wonders together, each using their own book. Whenever one player finds a wonder, the others also mark the item as "found." Share your curiosities too.

* **COMPETE.** Challenge a friend, racing to complete one chapter at a time. Or create teams and see who finishes first. If you like, switch opponents between chapters, inviting new people to join you.

PLAY WITH CARE

Wonder Hunt will take you out into the big, beautiful world in search of interesting phenomena. Here are a few things to keep in mind:

* **BE SAFE.** Sometimes wonder is so exciting that we get swept away! As you seek and find, be sure

to continue good safety practices like crossing streets carefully, waiting patiently in line, and engaging with people in safe ways.

* **BE RESPECTFUL.** There are wonders from many different places, peoples, and cultures. Some might be new to you. Be sure to approach the new-to-you things with care and respect. There might be culturally specific ways to touch the wonder (or not touch it) that you need to learn. Ask for help and be a good listener. Sometimes observing from afar can be best. If a wonder belongs to someone, ask permission before you get too close.

* **BE GENTLE.** Wonders have homes, just like people do. It's okay to remove some wonders—such as a seed pod on the ground—but not others—such as an item in a museum. Be aware of which wonders are living entities and leave them be.

THE 3 E'S OF WONDER HUNTING

1) Wonder is found *EVERYWHERE!*

2) Wonder happens *EVERY DAY.*

3) Wonder is for *EVERYONE,* including you!

When in doubt, ask yourself: *What would Aunt Lea do?* And remember, everything can be interesting. If you seek it, wonder is there waiting for you.

HAPPY HUNTING!

SIDEWALK FINDS

I am always surprised by the many kinds of small treasures waiting to be found on the ground. Sometimes I pick them up and take them home, like a colorful plastic bread tab, an interesting seed pod, or a penny. It's fun to collect pennies and then line them up on a windowsill back at home, from shiniest to darkest. It's also fun to just smile at a penny on the sidewalk and leave it there for the next person to find. Sometimes I just nod to the penny and think—*Hello, I see you*—and keep walking.

Did you know that the year stamped into the surface of a penny is the year the penny was minted? (A "mint" is a factory where the government manufactures money.) Each coin's birthyear is right there on its surface, in very fine print. So if you find a coin displaying the same year as the one in which you were born, then you and the coin are the same age! Will you mark this board's penny as "found" with the first penny you see, or will you wait for an extra-special penny such as a very shiny specimen or one listing your birthyear? It's up to you!

OH NO. A LOST BABY SOCK! I WONDER IF THE BABY HAS COLD TOES RIGHT NOW.

• • •

WHAT KIND OF BIRD DID THAT FEATHER COME FROM?

• • •

WHY DO SIDEWALKS HAVE GROOVES DIVIDING THE CONCRETE INTO SMALLER SQUARES?

sidewalk finds

1

Object:

Date: / /

Location: _____

I wonder:

2

Date: /   /

Location: _____

BREAD TAB

☐ Orange   ☐ Today's date   ☐ Your birthday

I wonder:

3

Date: /   /

Location: _____

SNAIL

☐ In motion   ☐ Still   ☐ Trail visible

I wonder:

4

Date: /   /

Location: _____

PENNY

☐ Heads up   ☐ Tails up   ☐ Very shiny

I wonder:

5

Date: /   /

Location: _____

FEATHER

☐ Blue   ☐ Attached to bird   ☐ Many

I wonder:

ITTEN

Date: / /

Location: _____

□ Plain   □ Patterned   □ On hand

wonder:

6

RUIT WITH CHILE SEASONING

Date: / /

Location: _____

□ Fruit stand   □ Mango   □ Served with a smile

wonder:

7

PUDDLE

Date: / /

Location: _____

□ Deep   □ Small   □ Jumped over

wonder:

8

BOTTLE CAP

Date: / /

Location: _____

□ Smashed   □ Soda   □ Message on underside

wonder:

9

10

Date: ___ / ___ / ___

Location: _____

☐ Friend   ☐ Neighbor   ☐ Cat

SOMEONE YOU KNOW

I wonder:

11

Date: ___ / ___ / ___

Location: _____

☐ $20 bill   ☐ Folded   ☐ Returned to owner

PAPER MONEY

I wonder:

12

Date: ___ / ___ / ___

Location: _____

☐ Small crack   ☐ Large crack   ☐ Tripped over

ROOTS UPTURNING CONCRETE

I wonder:

13

Date: ___ / ___ / ___

Location: _____

☐ Solid color   ☐ Striped   ☐ Polka dots

BABY SOCK

I wonder:

CRACKER

Date: /   /

Location: _____

☐ Whole   ☐ Cracked   ☐ Bitten

wonder:

LITTLE FREE LIBRARY

Date: /   /

Location: _____

☐ Stuffed full   ☐ Book donated   ☐ Good book taken

wonder:

UNTIED SHOELACE

Date: /   /

Location: _____

☐ You   ☐ Stranger   ☐ Someone you know

wonder:

FRUIT TREE

Date: /   /

Location: _____

☐ Fruit on branches   ☐ Fruit on ground   ☐ In bloom

wonder:

18

Date: /   /

Location: _____

SHOE PRINTS

☐ Pretty pattern   ☐ Your own   ☐ Matching yours

I wonder:

19

Date: /   /

Location: _____

SUNFLOWER SEEDS

☐ On ground   ☐ In bird feeder   ☐ On a sunflower

I wonder:

20

Date: /   /

Location: _____

FLOWER PETALS

☐ Cherry blossoms   ☐ In the air   ☐ Bougainvillea

I wonder:

21

Date: /   /

Location: _____

PUZZLE PIECE

☐ One piece   ☐ Corner piece   ☐ Many pieces

I wonder:

SMILE FROM A STRANGER

Date: / /

Location: _____

☐ Small smile ☐ Wide smile ☐ With eye contact

wonder:

ACORN

Date: / /

Location: _____

☐ With cap ☐ Acorn bread ☐ In squirrel's paws

wonder:

LOST EARRING

Date: / /

Location: _____

☐ Stud ☐ Dangle ☐ Clip-on

wonder:

FREE FURNITURE

Date: / /

Location: _____

☐ From friend ☐ From family ☐ Found on curb

wonder:

22

23

24

25

SO MANY SPHERES!

My favorite orb, without a doubt, is planet Earth. It is my home, your home, and—as far as we know—home to every living thing. Earth is located just the right distance from the Sun (another sphere I love) that it is not too hot or too cold here for life to thrive. I am fascinated by the fact that the Earth is so gargantuan I cannot see its spherical shape with my own eyes! When I look around, it appears flat, even though I know it is not. Go ahead: look around. See?

Photographs from outer space show me that Earth is shaped like a ball, but I also enjoy seeing the sphericality with my imagination. To do this, sometimes I take a moment and look down at the ground, toward my feet. Then, I think my way down into the Earth, through the layers of soil and rock and all the way through the hot molten core! I keep traveling through this imaginary tunnel until I pop up through the soil (or water!) on the opposite side of the planet. Isn't it strange and wonderful that there are people, animals, and plants far, far down below our feet, on the other side of the Earth?

I WONDER WHY A DROP OF DEW DOESN'T SOAK INTO THE LEAF IT IS SITTING ON.

• • •

WHEN I EAT SUSHI WITH TOBIKO, OR FLYING FISH EGGS, I NOTICE THAT THEY TASTE SALTY LIKE THE OCEAN.

• • •

WHAT IS THE SIZE OF THE LARGEST GUM BUBBLE THAT HAS EVER BEEN BLOWN?

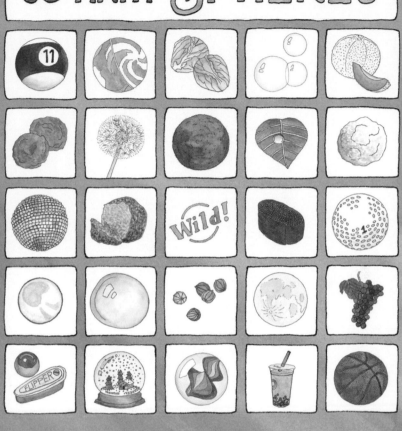

SO MANY SPHERES

Object:

Date: / /

Location: _____

I wonder:

Wild!

27

Date: /   /

Location: _____

☐ Colorful   ☐ Speckled   ☐ Opaque

MARBLE

I wonder:

28

Date: /   /

Location: _____

☐ Large   ☐ Huge!   ☐ Popped

GUM BUBBLE

I wonder:

29

Date: /   /

Location: _____

☐ On leaf   ☐ On flower   ☐ On spiderweb

DEW DROP

I wonder:

30

Date: /   /

Location: _____

☐ Full moon   ☐ Crescent moon   ☐ In daytime

MOON

I wonder:

GOLF BALL

Date: /   /

Location: _____

☐ Hole-in-one   ☐ At mini golf   ☐ Lost

wonder:

CORIANDER SEEDS

Date: /   /

Location: _____

☐ In jar   ☐ In food   ☐ On plant

wonder:

CANTALOUPE

Date: /   /

Location: _____

☐ Whole   ☐ Sliced   ☐ Balled

wonder:

PINBALL MACHINE

Date: /   /

Location: _____

☐ Analog   ☐ Digital   ☐ High score

wonder:

35

Date: / /

Location: _____

☐ Perfect ☐ Partial ☐ Made wish

DANDELION SEED HEAD

I wonder:

36

Date: / /

Location: _____

☐ Stripes ☐ Cue ball ☐ Bank shot

BILLIARD BALL

I wonder:

37

Date: / /

Location: _____

☐ Still ☐ Spinning ☐ Dancing

DISCO BALL

I wonder:

38

Date: / /

Location: _____

☐ White cheddar ☐ Messy fingers ☐ Fluorescent orange

CHEESE PUFF

I wonder:

NOWBALL

Date: / /

Location: _____

☐ Packed tight   ☐ Giant   ☐ Surprise attack

wonder:

ISH EGGS

Date: / /

Location: _____

☐ Tobiko   ☐ Caviar   ☐ In aquarium

wonder:

BRUSSELS SPROUTS

Date: / /

Location: _____

☐ Roasted   ☐ On the stalk   ☐ Sliced in half

wonder:

LOWN NOSE

Date: / /

Location: _____

☐ On clown   ☐ On you   ☐ For sale

wonder:

43

Date: / /

Location: _____

FALAFEL

☐ In pita ☐ Pickled vegetables ☐ With tahini sauce

I wonder:

44

Date: / /

Location: _____

TAPIOCA BALLS

☐ In bubble tea ☐ With fruit jelly ☐ On shaved ice

I wonder:

45

Date: / /

Location: _____

BUBBLES

☐ In bathtub ☐ Floating in air ☐ Mysterious source

I wonder:

46

Date: / /

Location: _____

GRAPES

☐ Purple ☐ On vine ☐ Raisins

I wonder:

SNOW GLOBE

Date: /   /

Location: _____

☐ Glitter   ☐ Winter scene   ☐ Souvenir

wonder:

PEARL

Date: /   /

Location: _____

☐ Earrings   ☐ Necklace   ☐ In oyster

wonder:

BOUNCY BALL

Date: /   /

Location:

☐ Solid color   ☐ Swirl design   ☐ In vending machine

wonder:

THREE-POINTER

Date: /   /

Location: _____

☐ Pickup game   ☐ Garage hoop   ☐ Pro game

wonder:

FLORA

Have you ever had pink lemonade? Have you ever seen a pink lemon?

My curiosity about the color of lemonade was first sparked when visiting my grandmother in the Arizona desert. After making a pitcher of lemonade, she drizzled in some syrup and gave it a good stir. It changed from light yellow to bright pink! I soon learned that the magenta color came from the fruit of the *Opuntia* cactus, commonly referred to as prickly pear, nopal, or paddle cactus. *Opuntia* grew in my grandparents' backyard, front yard, side yard, and up and down all the mountains and arroyos nearby.

Sometimes the plants would be 100 percent green—thick spiky stems in the shape of Ping-Pong paddles. In summer: big pink blossoms ready for bees! Soon after, I would find prickly pink fruits where the flowers used to be. The pulpy, sweet packages had gathered up the sun and the rain of monsoon season, offering it to the critters of the desert. This included the human critters who could carefully harvest some, chop them up, and boil them down into a beautiful, natural food-coloring. Not all pink lemonade is colored with prickly pears, but my favorite kind certainly is.

HOW DO THE MICROSCOPIC CHLOROPLASTS INSIDE PLANTS TURN SUNSHINE INTO FOOD?

• • •

A SEED PACKET CAN BE A MUSICAL INSTRUMENT IF I SHAKE IT!

• • •

I WONDER IF I JUST POLLINATED THESE LILIES BY STICKING MY NOSE IN TO SMELL THEM.

FLORA

Object:

Date: /   /

Location: _____

I wonder:

Wild!

52

Date: / /

Location: _____

☐ Saw it ☐ Big thud ☐ Ate it

FRUIT FALLING FROM TREE

I wonder:

53

Date: / /

Location: _____

☐ Three-leaf ☐ Four-leaf ☐ In bloom

CLOVER

I wonder:

54

Date: / /

Location: _____

☐ Blackberries ☐ Thimbleberries ☐ Huckleberries

WILD BERRIES

I wonder:

55

Date: / /

Location: _____

☐ Planted by me ☐ Avocado pit ☐ Community garden

SPROUTING SEED

I wonder:

GREENHOUSE

Date: / /

Location: _____

☐ At a park ☐ Backyard ☐ At a farm

wonder:

TREE SWING

Date: / /

Location: _____

☐ Wood ☐ Tire ☐ Over water

wonder:

WILDFLOWER

Date: / /

Location: _____

☐ Just a few ☐ A field full ☐ You know its name

wonder:

BEAUTIFUL BARK

Date: / /

Location: _____

☐ Birch ☐ Madrone ☐ Looks like puzzle pieces

wonder:

60

Date: /   /

Location: _____

YOUR STATE FLOWER

☐ In a park   ☐ In a yard   ☐ In the wild

I wonder:

61

Date: /   /

Location: _____

BAREFOOT IN THE GRASS

☐ Soft   ☐ Prickly   ☐ Picnic

I wonder:

62

Date: /   /

Location: _____

FUZZY PLANT

☐ Lamb's ear   ☐ African violet   ☐ Surface of a peach

I wonder:

63

Date: /   /

Location: _____

CHERRY TOMATO

☐ Yellow   ☐ With stem   ☐ Still growing

I wonder:

PLANT FIBER GARMENT

Date: /   /

Location: _____

☐ Cotton   ☐ Linen   ☐ Hemp

wonder:

SEED PACKET

Date: /   /

Location: _____

☐ Beautiful art   ☐ Unopened   ☐ Opened

wonder:

MORNING GLORY
104
SEEDS

COLLARD GREENS

Date: /   /

Location: _____

☐ Growing   ☐ In cooking pot   ☐ On your plate

wonder:

ACT OF POLLINATION

Date: /   /

Location: _____

☐ Bee   ☐ Butterfly   ☐ Hummingbird

wonder:

68

Date: / /

KALE

Location: _____

☐ Baby   ☐ Dino   ☐ Covered in aphids

I wonder:

69

Date: / /

SAFFRON

Location: _____

☐ In spice jar   ☐ In paella   ☐ On flower

I wonder:

70

Date: / /

WILTING FLOWERS

Location: _____

☐ Pretty vase   ☐ Petals on table   ☐ Rotten scent

I wonder:

71

Date: / /

NOTEBOOK PAPER

Location: _____

☐ Crumpled   ☐ College-ruled   ☐ Completed homework

I wonder:

PRICKLY PEAR CACTUS

Date: /   /

Location: _____

72

☐ Blossoming   ☐ Fruiting   ☐ In lemonade

wonder:

GARDEN TROWEL

Date: /   /

Location: _____

73

☐ In use   ☐ Well-loved   ☐ Wooden handle

wonder:

HAY BALE

Date: /   /

Location: _____

74

☐ In field   ☐ At party   ☐ Cylindrical shape

wonder:

PAPYRUS

Date: /   /

Location: _____

75

☐ Plant growing   ☐ Made into paper   ☐ In museum

wonder:

FAUNA

I don't have any pets, but there are animals I love. A covey of quail babies scurrying after their mother is charming to watch. Sometimes beautiful moths visit me in the evening, basking in my electric lighting from the other side of the window. I plant flowers in my yard that I know the bees will love.

My favorite animal-human duo consists of my bright, college-student cousin and her adorable, loving black Lab, Juno. Most of the time, Juno is busy working, so I am careful not to distract her with head rubs. I know Juno is on duty when she is wearing her vest that says "Autism Service Dog." Each autistic person experiences the world around them in their own unique way. For many, social interaction can be challenging. To thrive, my cousin needs her service dog. And Juno is allowed to go everywhere she goes— to class, to the grocery store, into restaurants. If my cousin is overstimulated and, for example, pumping her arms back and forth, Juno will notice and imme- diately interrupt the behavior by catching my cousin's attention. Juno might even jump into her lap! Juno is smart, curious, and pays close attention. If Juno were a human, she would be very good at this book!

WHO FIRST DISCOVERED THAT A FEATHER WOULD MAKE A GOOD WRITING IMPLEMENT?

• • •

CAN THE FISH SEE THE HUNGRY PELICAN COMING WHEN IT DIVES FROM THE SKY?

• • •

I WONDER WHAT THE SHEEP WHO GREW THE WOOL FOR MY SWEATER LOOKS LIKE.

FAUNA

Object:

Date: /   /

Location: _____

wonder:

77

Date: /   /

Location: _____

☐ Zoo   ☐ Wild   ☐ Feather only

PEACOCK

I wonder:

78

Date: /   /

Location: _____

☐ Goat   ☐ Horse   ☐ Chicken

PETTING ZOO

I wonder:

79

Date: /   /

Location: _____

☐ Has a name   ☐ At pet store   ☐ Feeding time

GOLDFISH

I wonder:

80

Date: /   /

Location: _____

☐ Striped   ☐ Wild   ☐ Molting

SNAKE

I wonder:

RACCOON

Date: /   /

Location: _____

☐ Rummaging through garbage   ☐ In yard   ☐ Running

wonder:

YOUR STATE BIRD

Date: /   /

Location: _____

☐ In flight   ☐ In a tree   ☐ Singing

wonder:

PARENT & BABY TOGETHER

Date: /   /

Location: _____

☐ Kangaroos   ☐ Ducks   ☐ Humans

wonder:

MILK

Date: /   /

Location: _____

☐ Baby bottle   ☐ Inside a cow   ☐ With cookies

wonder:

CREAMERY
ORGANIC

85

Date: /   /

Location: _____

☐ Near biscuits   ☐ Empty   ☐ Local honey

HONEY BEAR

I wonder:

86

Date: /   /

Location: _____

☐ Pelican   ☐ Seagull   ☐ A successful catch!

WATER BIRD DIVING

I wonder:

87

Date: /   /

Location: _____

☐ In soil   ☐ In compost   ☐ On sidewalk

EARTHWORM

I wonder:

88

Date: /   /

Location: _____

☐ Yours   ☐ Loved one's   ☐ A broken bone

X-RAY

I wonder:

BARN

Date: / /

Location: _____

☐ Huge ☐ Leaning ☐ Red

wonder:

KATYDID

Date: / /

Location: _____

☐ Loud ☐ Lots ☐ Well-camouflaged

wonder:

WOOL SWEATER

Date: / /

Location: _____

☐ Sheep ☐ Llama ☐ Cashmere goat

wonder:

FEATHER PEN

Date: / /

Location: _____

☐ In use ☐ In museum ☐ Made your own

wonder:

93

Date: ___ / ___ / ___

Location: _____

MOTH

☐ On window   ☐ Near light bulb   ☐ At night

I wonder:

94

Date: ___ / ___ / ___

Location: _____

SERVICE DOG

☐ Labrador retriever   ☐ Busy working   ☐ Wearing vest

I wonder:

95

Date: ___ / ___ / ___

Location: _____

FIREFLIES

☐ Daytime   ☐ Nighttime   ☐ Cluster

I wonder:

96

Date: ___ / ___ / ___

Location: _____

BIRD EGG

☐ Robin   ☐ Chicken   ☐ Cracked

I wonder:

BISON

Date: /   /

Location: _____

☐ In the wild   ☐ On a U.S. nickel   ☐ In a national park

wonder:

SAND DOLLAR

Date: /   /

Location: _____

☐ On beach   ☐ In collection   ☐ Tiny

wonder:

ANIMAL TRACKS

Date: /   /

Location: _____

☐ In sand   ☐ In dirt   ☐ In snow

wonder:

TATTOO OF AN ANIMAL

Date: /   /

Location: _____

☐ Pet   ☐ Insect   ☐ Sea creature

wonder:

COOL TOOLS

I strapped a snorkel to my face for the first time when I was about seven years old. I was nervous, and excited. The good part: I was going to be able to breathe underwater like a fish! The scary part: I was going to be underwater with all the fish! I summoned my courage and plunged my face below the surface. I instructed myself: BREATHE. In my mind, I understood how a snorkel worked. A plastic tube carried air from above the water down to my mouth under the water. But even though this tool made perfect sense in my mind, my body still felt so strange!

Breathing underwater felt uncomfortable and new. I could feel my heart beating fast. And then, soon enough, I got used to it. I learned that I could trust the snorkel. A few dozen kicks of my swim fins and I was breathing easy, swimming with bright orange Garibaldi, pausing to watch a school of sardines flash past me, and admiring the way the sun rays cascade through towers of kelp. I bet you, too, have a tool you have learned to trust. Can you think of one now?

WHAT IS THE NAME OF THE BIG CONTRAPTION AT THE OPTOMETRIST'S OFFICE THAT GIVES ME MY NEW EYEGLASSES PRESCRIPTION?

• • •

WHY DO APPLE SLICES TASTE BETTER WHEN THEY ARE CUT WITH THE SPECIAL APPLE SLICER AT MY AUNT'S HOUSE?

• • •

THE ITSY PAPER CIRCLES LEFT OVER FROM THE HOLE PUNCH LOOK LIKE TINY MOONS!

COOL TOOLS

Object:

Date: /   /

Location: _____

I wonder:

Wild!

102

Date: / /

Location: _____

☐ Lamp ☐ Blender ☐ Electric car

ELECTRICITY

I wonder:

103

Date: / /

Location: _____

☐ Home ☐ Restaurant ☐ Hand-crank

PASTA MACHINE

I wonder:

104

Date: / /

Location: _____

☐ In use ☐ Antique ☐ Known feather type

FEATHER DUSTER

I wonder:

105

Date: / /

Location: _____

☐ Urban view ☐ Wild animal view ☐ Opera glasses

BINOCULARS

I wonder:

HIMBLE

Date: /   /

Location: _____

☐ Metal   ☐ Plastic   ☐ In use

wonder:

ELLOWS

Date: /   /

Location: _____

☐ In use   ☐ Near fireplace   ☐ In museum

wonder:

IND DIRECTION NSTRUMENT

Date: /   /

Location: _____

☐ Weathervane   ☐ Wind sock   ☐ Wet finger

wonder:

HOROPTER

Date: /   /

Location: _____

☐ New glasses   ☐ Updated prescription   ☐ First time

wonder:

110

Date: / /

Location: _____

ASTRONAUT SUIT

☐ On TV ☐ In book ☐ Costume

I wonder:

111

Date: / /

Location: _____

STICKY NOTE

☐ Reminder ☐ Bookmark ☐ Kind message

I wonder:

street sweeping TOMORROW!!

112

Date: / /

Location: _____

APPLE SLICER

☐ In use ☐ Vintage ☐ At aunt's house

I wonder:

113

Date: / /

Location: _____

COPY MACHINE

☐ Black and white ☐ Color ☐ Double-sided printing

I wonder:

IOLE PUNCH

Date: /   /

Location: _____

☐ Craft project   ☐ Gift tag making   ☐ Chads on floor

wonder:

LOBE

Date: /   /

Location: _____

☐ Moon   ☐ Earth   ☐ Raised relief

wonder:

TETHOSCOPE

Date: /   /

Location: _____

☐ Toy   ☐ On doctor's neck   ☐ On your chest

wonder:

LANISPHERE
TAR MAP

Date: /   /

Location: _____

☐ In use   ☐ Learned to use   ☐ Constellation found

wonder:

118

Date: ___ / ___ / ___

Location: _____

SOMETHING WITH GEARS

☐ Bicycle   ☐ Machine   ☐ Factory tour

I wonder:

119

Date: ___ / ___ / ___

Location: _____

ARROWHEAD

☐ On ground   ☐ Has a story   ☐ Made by your relation

I wonder:

120

Date: ___ / ___ / ___

Location: _____

BRAILLE DOTS

☐ Paper   ☐ In elevator   ☐ On airplane

I wonder:

121

Date: ___ / ___ / ___

Location: _____

PEPPER MILL

☐ Wooden mill   ☐ Plastic mill   ☐ At restaurant

I wonder:

NORKEL

Date: /   /

Location: _____

☐ In use   ☐ On you   ☐ Saw something cool!

wonder:

IBRARY CARD

Date: /   /

Location: _____

☐ Brand-new   ☐ Well-used   ☐ Summer reading program

wonder:

New York
Public
Library
KNOWLEDGE IS POWER

EFT-HANDED TOOL

Date: /   /

Location: _____

☐ Scissors   ☐ Measuring tape   ☐ Pruning shears

wonder:

ANUAL EGGBEATER

Date: /   /

Location: _____

☐ In use   ☐ Broken   ☐ At antique store

wonder:

TINY THINGS

Some tiny things are abundant, like grains of salt, poppy seeds on a bagel, or fennel seeds in a bowl of mukhwas. Some small items, like clothes buttons, are easy to find. Still other little bits can be hard to find and easy to lose, such as sea glass. When I was a child, every time I lost another tooth, I would put it into a tiny plastic treasure chest for safe keeping. The itsy orange chest was a free prize from the dentist's office. I loved it. But then I lost the whole chest!

Some tiny things are made more than found. Have you ever had silver dollar pancakes? They are a delightful breakfast. Instead of pouring a few big puddles of batter on the griddle, you spoon lots of tiny puddles, each one the size of a silver dollar coin. They cook faster than big pancakes, so you must keep an eye on them to keep them from burning. Part of the fun of these tiny pancakes is that you get to eat a big stack of them since they're so small. It's fun to try to balance them in a very tall tower!

IF I PLANT THE SEEDS FROM THIS POPPY SEED BAGEL, WILL THEY GROW INTO FLOWERS?

• • •

I WONDER HOW A SNOWSTORM CREATES SO MANY DIFFERENT SNOWFLAKE SHAPES AND PATTERNS.

• • •

WHO CAN TEACH ME HOW TO REPLACE A MISSING BUTTON USING A NEEDLE AND THREAD?

tiny things

Object: _____

Date: ____ / ____ / ____

Location: _____

wonder: _____

Wild!

127 SPRINKLES

Date: / /

Location: _____

☐ Rainbow ☐ Chocolate ☐ Frozen yogurt

I wonder:

128 MAP PINS

Date: / /

Location: _____

☐ Spheres ☐ Flags ☐ Numbered

I wonder:

129 POPPY SEEDS

Date: / /

Location: _____

☐ Bagel ☐ Lemon cake ☐ Gardening

I wonder:

130 ALPHABET NOODLES

Date: / /

Location: _____

☐ Dry ☐ Soup ☐ Spelled your name

I wonder:

RY BEANS

Date: /   /

Location: _____

☐ In storage   ☐ Soaking   ☐ For Lotería

wonder:

UMMINGBIRD

Date: /   /

Location: _____

☐ Hovering   ☐ Beak in flower   ☐ Ruby-throated

wonder:

EARS

Date: /   /

Location: _____

☐ Friend   ☐ Family   ☐ Your own

wonder:

ABY TOES

Date: /   /

Location: _____

☐ Newborn   ☐ Soft   ☐ Cute

wonder:

135

Date: / /

Location: _____

☐ Tall tower ☐ Homemade ☐ Gluten-free

SILVER DOLLAR PANCAKES

I wonder:

136

Date: / /

Location: _____

☐ Sea salt ☐ Pink ☐ Flaky

A GRAIN OF SALT

I wonder:

137

Date: / /

Location: _____

☐ Peppermint ☐ Spearmint ☐ Wintergreen

MINTS

I wonder:

138

Date: / /

Location: _____

☐ Restaurant ☐ Home ☐ Market

MUKHWAS

I wonder:

PUNCTUATION MARKS

Date: / /

Location: _____

☐ Ellipsis   ☐ Semicolon   ☐ Interrobang?

wonder:

DANDELION SEED

Date: / /

Location: _____

☐ On seed head   ☐ Floating   ☐ Under microscope

wonder:

140

LOST BUTTON

Date: / /

Location: _____

☐ Found one   ☐ Saw it happen   ☐ Sewed it back on

wonder:

141

FINE PRINT

Date: / /

Location: _____

☐ Clothes tag   ☐ Ingredients list   ☐ Handwriting

wonder:

142

MENS M MEDIUM
65% POLYESTER
35% COTTON
MADE IN
CAMBODIA
STYLE# PT12F3

143

Date: / /

ANT

Location: _____

☐ Alone   ☐ In a long trail   ☐ In kitchen

I wonder:

144

Date: / /

TOASTED O'S

Location: _____

☐ Floating   ☐ Crunchy   ☐ Soggy

I wonder:

145

Date: / /

TWINKLY LIGHTS

Location: _____

☐ White   ☐ Multi-colored   ☐ Blinking

I wonder:

146

Date: / /

TINY HEXAGON TILE FLOOR

Location: _____

☐ Black and white   ☐ All white   ☐ Restroom

I wonder:

MICROSCOPE

Date: /   /

Location: _____

☐ Sea water   ☐ Plant matter   ☐ Critters

147

wonder:

LADYBUG

Date: /   /

Location: _____

☐ In a cluster   ☐ Wings visible   ☐ Eating aphids

148

wonder:

PAPER UMBRELLA

Date: /   /

Location: _____

☐ Open   ☐ Closed   ☐ In beverage

149

wonder:

SNOWFLAKE

Date: /   /

Location: _____

☐ In the air   ☐ On your palm   ☐ On your tongue

150

wonder:

SURPRISE!

Some surprises—such as thunderstorms—I love. Others—like unexpected dollops of nose-stinging wasabi hiding inside a maki roll—I could do without! But I welcome other unexpected delights, such as home-baked cookies at my doorstep and flowers growing out of cracks in the sidewalk. I also love it when one of my favorite songs suddenly plays in public or at a friend's house. Why does the song sound even better when I'm not expecting it?

One time, I received a wonderful surprise that I didn't even know was possible. I cannot remember exactly what I was making. A cake? A quiche? But when I tapped the raw egg to crack its shell, letting the inside pour out, there were two yolks instead of one! I laughed out loud, even though I was alone in my kitchen. I felt like I had won the grand prize in a contest I didn't realize I had entered. It made my day. My great-grandmother was a twin. I wonder if her parents knew they were going to have twins or if it happened more like my egg. Surprise! Not one, but two!

WHEN COOKING FROM A RECIPE, DOES A TWO-YOLK EGG COUNT AS ONE EGG OR TWO?

• • •

WHY DO I ALWAYS FEEL LIKE A SLIGHTLY DIFFERENT PERSON AFTER A HAIRCUT?

• • •

I WONDER IF I COULD BAKE MY OWN FORTUNE COOKIES AT HOME AND WRITE THE FORTUNES MYSELF?

Object: _____

Date: _____ / _____ / _____

Location: _____

I wonder:

152

Date: /   /

Location: _____

☐ You laughed   ☐ You gasped   ☐ You told someone

TWO-YOLK EGG

I wonder:

153

Date: /   /

Location: _____

☐ Unusual name   ☐ Overheard   ☐ Name tag

SOMEONE WITH YOUR NAME

I wonder:

HELLO
my name is
? ? ?

154

Date: /   /

Location: _____

☐ Okay   ☐ Too spicy   ☐ Delicious

UNEXPECTED WASABI

I wonder:

155

Date: /   /

Location: _____

☐ On clothes   ☐ On skin   ☐ Close call

POOPED ON BY A PIGEON

I wonder:

WINNING RAFFLE TICKET

Date: / /

Location: _____

☐ You   ☐ Stranger   ☐ Someone you know

wonder:

REPURPOSED PLANTER

Date: / /

Location: _____

☐ Toilet   ☐ Tin can   ☐ Drawer

wonder:

RAINBOW

Date: / /

Location: _____

☐ Single   ☐ Double   ☐ In waterfall spray

wonder:

CANADIAN PENNY

Date: / /

Location: _____

☐ In Canada   ☐ Outside Canada   ☐ Near maple tree

wonder:

160

Date: / /

Location: _____

FORTUNE COOKIE

☐ Desirable fortune ☐ Lucky numbers included ☐ Already came true

I wonder:

? ? ?

161

Date: / /

Location: _____

SOMEONE ELSE'S MAIL IN YOUR MAILBOX

☐ Nearby ☐ Far away ☐ You know them

I wonder:

To: Someone Else
Wrong Place
12345

162

Date: / /

Location: _____

WATERMELON JELLY BEANS

☐ Eaten whole ☐ Red inside ☐ Shared with friend

I wonder:

163

Date: / /

Location: _____

NEW HAIRCUT

☐ Shorter ☐ New style ☐ Bangs

I wonder:

AIL

Date: ___ / ___ / ___

Location: _____

☐ Loud ☐ Geometric shape ☐ On windshield

wonder:

NEXPECTED GIFT

Date: ___ / ___ / ___

Location: _____

☐ Thoughtful ☐ A little something ☐ Anonymous giver

wonder:

DVENT CALENDAR

Date: ___ / ___ / ___

Location: _____

☐ Took turns opening ☐ Double door ☐ Completed

wonder:

AGIC TRICK

Date: ___ / ___ / ___

Location: _____

☐ At show ☐ On sidewalk ☐ Performed by you

wonder:

168

Date: /   /

Location: _____

CHANGE HIDING IN COUCH

☐ Less than $1   ☐ More than $1   ☐ Enough to buy a treat

I wonder:

169

Date: /   /

Location: _____

HAPPY ACCIDENT

☐ Noticed immediately   ☐ Smiled   ☐ Took time to appreciate

I wonder:

OOPS. AWESOME!

170

Date: /   /

Location: _____

INSECT HIDING

☐ Under a rock   ☐ In fruit   ☐ In vegetable

I wonder:

171

Date: /   /

Location: _____

PERFECTLY TIMED SIGNAL

☐ Walk signal   ☐ Traffic light   ☐ Railroad crossing

I wonder:

ESTING DOLLS

Date: /   /

Location: _____

☐ People   ☐ Animals   ☐ Hand-painted

wonder:

LOWER GROWING OUT F A CRACK

Date: /   /

Location: _____

☐ Sidewalk   ☐ Parking lot   ☐ Wall

wonder:

IÑATA

Date: /   /

Location: _____

☐ At party   ☐ In store   ☐ You broke it open

wonder:

OOL OLD CAR N THE ROAD

Date: /   /

Location: _____

☐ Bright color   ☐ Convertible   ☐ Over 100 years old

wonder:

LET'S PLAY!

Almost anything can be a toy if we approach it play-fully. These kinds of "found toys" can hide right under our noses. If I am at a diner waiting for my toast to arrive, sometimes I play tic-tac-toe with the pink and white sugar packets at the table. If I am walking under a maple tree at the precise moment when a little "helicopter" seed pod spins down at me like a balle-rina, I smile. After it hits the ground, I can toss it back into the air and watch it twirl again.

Sometimes I wake up feeling playful about my clothes, pairing, say, colorful polka dot pants with a black-and-white striped shirt. Have you ever played with your socks in this way? Since socks are sold in pairs, it is easy to think that those two socks should always be worn together. However, it can be fun to mix and match socks instead, playing with different combi-nations of color and pattern. I like to think of it as two different socks having a great conversation, just like two good friends might. If they could talk, what would your various sock patterns say to each other?

IS THERE ANYTHING NEARBY I CAN PLAY WITH WHILE I WAIT IN THIS LONG LINE?

• • •

BOWLING SHOES ARE AWESOME. COULD I WEAR BOWLING SHOES AS MY REGULAR SHOES?

• • •

I WONDER HOW MANY TIMES THOSE SKATERS PRACTICED BEFORE DOING THAT TRICK SO WELL.

LET'S PLAY

Object:

Date: ___ / ___ / ___

Location: _____

wonder:

Wild!

177

Date: /   /

Location: _____

PUZZLE CUBE

☐ Already solved ☐ Gave up ☐ Watched it be solved

I wonder:

178

Date: /   /

Location: _____

BOWLING SHOES

☐ One-color ☐ Two-color ☐ Three-color

I wonder:

179

Date: /   /

Location: _____

ARCADE VIDEO GAME

☐ Joystick ☐ Steering wheel ☐ Buttons

I wonder

A

B

180

Date: /   /

Location: _____

SOMEONE FINGER PAINTING

☐ Messy ☐ Big mess ☐ Huge mess

I wonder

FINGER PAINT

FING PAIN

KITTEN

Date: /   /

Location: _____

☐ Chasing   ☐ Jumping   ☐ Napping

wonder:

SUPERHERO CAPE
IN PUBLIC

Date: /   /

Location: _____

☐ On adult   ☐ On Halloween   ☐ Not on Halloween

wonder:

WEARING MISMATCHED
SOCKS

Date: /   /

Location: _____

☐ Accidentally   ☐ Purposefully   ☐ Hidden under pants

wonder:

OVERHEARD: "KING ME!"

Date: /   /

Location: _____

☐ Close game   ☐ Plastic checkers   ☐ Wooden checkers

wonder:

185

Date: /   /

Location: _____

☐ Seen   ☐ Played in   ☐ Being built

TREEHOUSE

I wonder:

186

Date: /   /

Location: _____

☐ She   ☐ He   ☐ They

SNOWPERSON

I wonder:

187

Date: /   /

Location: _____

☐ Chandelier crystals   ☐ Hanging in window   ☐ Rainbow on you

PRISMS CASTING RAINBOWS

I wonder:

188

Date: /   /

Location: _____

☐ Up high   ☐ Down low   ☐ Too slow

HIGH FIVE

I wonder:

UMP ROPE

Date: / /

Location: _____

☐ In action ☐ Double Dutch ☐ Two-color

wonder:

NSIDE FORT

Date: / /

Location: _____

☐ Cushions ☐ Furniture ☐ Snacks

wonder:

MPRESSIVE
KATEBOARD TRICK

Date: / /

Location: _____

☐ Very fancy ☐ Good try ☐ Someone you know

wonder:

ANCING SHOES

Date: / /

Location: _____

☐ Ballet ☐ Tap ☐ High heels

wonder:

193

Date: ___ / ___ / ___

Location: _____

MAPLE SEED PODS

☐ Twirling in air ☐ On tree ☐ On ground

I wonder:

194

Date: ___ / ___ / ___

Location: _____

BULL'S-EYE

☐ Darts ☐ Archery ☐ Lucky

I wonder:

195

Date: ___ / ___ / ___

Location: _____

NATURE FORT

☐ Beach ☐ Forest ☐ Backyard

I wonder:

196

Date: ___ / ___ / ___

Location: _____

COMPLETED CROSSWORD PUZZLE

☐ In pencil ☐ In pen ☐ By you

I wonder:

MANCALA GAME

Date: / /

Location: _____

☐ Glass pieces   ☐ Stones   ☐ Beans

wonder:

197

OCARINA

Date: / /

Location: _____

☐ Clay   ☐ Wood   ☐ Plastic

wonder:

198

DAYDREAM

Date: / /

Location: _____

☐ Fantastical   ☐ About the future   ☐ Lost track of time

wonder:

199

OVERHEARD:
"RACE YOU!"

Date: / /

Location: _____

☐ Children   ☐ Adults   ☐ You won

wonder:

200

RACE YOU!

FOOD FOR THOUGHT

This fall I discovered a fig tree across the street from my home. I have lived in my neighborhood of Oakland, California, for three years, but this was my first time noticing this tree. How did I miss it last fall? Was this the first time the tree fruited, or was it just the first time I noticed the fruit? It is a public tree, so anyone is welcome to pick and enjoy the tree-ripened fruits. So, during fig season, whenever I wanted a snack, I simply stepped out my front door and visited the tree.

Some foods arrive ready-to-go, like tree-ripe figs. Others are a labor of love to prepare, such as the patterned edge of an empanada, the braid of a loaf of challah, or the hand-woven ketupat. Originally from Indonesia, these hand-crafted pouches are woven from palm fronds and packed with rice. The rice expands and compresses as it cooks inside the patterned packet, creating a delicious texture. You peel the packet like a little present and eat the rice cake inside. Is there something special you love to eat that takes time and care to prepare?

I WONDER HOW THEY GET THE ROSE FLAVOR OUT OF THE ROSE.

• • •

DOES THE HUMMINGBIRD KNOW THIS BIRD FEEDER IS NOT A REAL FLOWER?

• • •

WHAT MAKES SOME PLANTS SAFE TO EAT WHILE OTHERS ARE NOT?

FOOD FOR THOUGHT

Object:

Date: / /

Location: _____

I wonder:

Wild!

202

Date: ___ / ___ / ___

Location: _____

FINGER FOOD

☐ Empanada   ☐ Ants on a log   ☐ Bolani

I wonder:

203

Date: ___ / ___ / ___

Location: _____

SANDWICH CUT ON DIAGONAL

☐ Whole-grain bread   ☐ Crust removed   ☐ Hold the mayo

I wonder:

204

Date: ___ / ___ / ___

Location: _____

DURIAN

☐ At market   ☐ Smelled it   ☐ Tasted it

I wonder:

205

Date: ___ / ___ / ___

Location: _____

CHEWY TREAT

☐ Rose lokum   ☐ Red-bean mochi   ☐ Salted caramel

I wonder:

HOMEMADE MUFFINS

Date: /   /

Location: _____

☐ Blueberry   ☐ Carrot   ☐ Cornbread

wonder:

KETUPAT

Date: /   /

Location: _____

☐ Empty pouches for sale   ☐ You wove pouch   ☐ Picture of

wonder:

OKRA

Date: /   /

Location: _____

☐ Roasted   ☐ Deep fried   ☐ Slimy

wonder:

BRAIDED BREAD

Date: /   /

Location: _____

☐ Challah   ☐ Savory   ☐ Sweet

wonder:

210

Date: / /

Location: _____

BARBECUE IN PUBLIC

☐ Smells good ☐ Party ☐ Corn on cob

I wonder:

211

Date: / /

Location: _____

COMPOST

☐ Pile ☐ Worm bin ☐ Bucket in kitchen

I wonder:

212

Date: / /

Location: _____

HIDDEN PICTURE
IN FOOD

☐ In burnt toast ☐ Face ☐ Creature

I wonder:

213

Date: / /

Location: _____

GROCERY CART THAT
VEERS TO ONE SIDE

☐ Annoying ☐ Entertaining ☐ Broken wheel

I wonder:

DIBLE FLOWERS

Date: / /

Location: _____

☐ In salad   ☐ Candied petals   ☐ Flavor in baked good

wonder:

URPLE FOOD

Date: / /

Location: _____

☐ Fig   ☐ Carrot   ☐ Taro

wonder:

GIFT OF FOOD

Date: / /

Location: _____

☐ Meal program   ☐ Senior delivery   ☐ From a neighbor

wonder:

NION MAKING OMEONE CRY

Date: / /

Location: _____

☐ Just a little   ☐ Needed a tissue   ☐ Tears down cheeks

wonder:

218

Date: /   /

Location: _____

FOOD ON A STICK

☐ Deep fried   ☐ At festival   ☐ At campfire

I wonder:

219

Date: /   /

Location: _____

GARNISH

☐ Parsley   ☐ Pickled   ☐ Decorative

I wonder:

220

Date: /   /

Location: _____

CHILE

☐ Mild   ☐ Hot   ☐ Habañero

I wonder:

221

Date: /   /

Location: _____

CHOPSTICKS

☐ First time   ☐ Still learning   ☐ Highly skilled

I wonder:

KIMCHI

Date: / /

Location: _____

☐ At home   ☐ At restaurant   ☐ Spicy

wonder:

BIRD FEEDER

Date: / /

Location: _____

☐ Full of seeds   ☐ Bird enjoying   ☐ For hummingbirds

wonder:

FRUIT PIE

Date: / /

Location: _____

☐ Apple   ☐ Cherry   ☐ Peach

wonder:

WHOLE SPICES

Date: / /

Location: _____

☐ Cardamom   ☐ Star anise   ☐ Peppercorns

wonder:

PATTERNS ARE EVERYWHERE

Patterns are pervasive. Big or small, detailed or simple, they are all around us. Humans make them. Other animals make them. Forces of nature make them. The planets swing around the Sun in circles just like a ring swings around my finger. Colorful rock formations stack up into geologic layers like a layered cake. A cross-sectional slice of a lotus root reminds me of a stained-glass window I saw in a cathedral in France. The small raised dots on the surface of a sea urchin shell feel a lot like Braille.

I don't know if I am correct, but I have a theory—a thought, an idea, a good guess. One time I was travelling over a creek on a country road. On both sides of the entrance to the small bridge were rectangular "caution" signs with diagonal yellow and black stripes. I knew they were warning me to be careful as I crossed. I'd seen these many times before. This time, I suddenly realized that they looked like a giant, abstracted version of a tiny stinging animal: a wasp! My theory is that the sign designers chose this color scheme because wasps require caution too. What do you think?

I WONDER WHY BEES BUILD THEIR HONEYCOMB HOME IN A HEXAGONAL PATTERN.

• • •

WHAT DID THIS SEA URCHIN SHELL LOOK LIKE WHEN ITS INHABITANT WAS STILL ALIVE?

• • •

CAN I FIND A VIDEO SHOWING HOW MARBLEIZED PAPER IS MADE?

PATTERNS ARE EVERYWHERE

Object:

Date: /   /

Location: _____

wonder:

Date: / /

Location: _____

FRIENDSHIP BRACELET

☐ "V" pattern   ☐ "X" pattern   ☐ Diagonal stripes

I wonder

Date: / /

Location: _____

HONEYCOMB

☐ Chewy   ☐ On toast   ☐ In bee box frame

I wonder

Date: / /

Location: _____

MUSHROOM GILLS

☐ In garden   ☐ Wild   ☐ At farmer's market

I wonder

Date: / /

Location: _____

RAINDROP RIPPLES

☐ Puddle   ☐ Pond   ☐ Fountain

I wonder

MOSAIC

Date: /   /

Location: _____

☐ Ceramic   ☐ Stone   ☐ Glass

wonder:

SPIDERWEB

Date: /   /

Location: _____

☐ Spider visible   ☐ Flies trapped   ☐ Surprising location

wonder:

SECURITY ENVELOPE

Date: /   /

Location: _____

☐ Plaid   ☐ Squiggles   ☐ Blue

wonder:

FIBONACCI SPIRAL

Date: /   /

Location: _____

☐ Romanesco   ☐ Sunflower head   ☐ Shell

wonder:

235

Date: ___/___/___

Location: _____

☐ In tide pool ☐ Far from ocean ☐ Held carefully

SEA URCHIN SHELL

I wonder:

236

Date: ___/___/___

Location: _____

☐ On paper ☐ On glass ☐ Your own

FINGERPRINTS

I wonder:

237

Date: ___/___/___

Location: _____

☐ Shirt ☐ Kilt ☐ Pajamas

PLAID

I wonder:

238

Date: ___/___/___

Location: _____

☐ Path ☐ Street ☐ Patio

COBBLESTONE

I wonder:

CAUTION ROAD SIGN

Date: /   /

Location: _____

☐ Diagonal stripes   ☐ Chevron pattern   ☐ Looks like a wasp

wonder:

MANY LAYERS

Date: /   /

Location: _____

☐ Cake   ☐ Rocks   ☐ Clothing

wonder:

BEAUTIFUL CROSS SECTION

Date: /   /

Location: _____

☐ Lotus root   ☐ Star fruit   ☐ Cinnamon roll

wonder:

MUDCRACKS

Date: /   /

Location: _____

☐ Tiny cracks   ☐ Small cracks   ☐ Large cracks

wonder:

243

Date: /   /

Location: _____

BRAIDED HAIR

☐ Cornrows   ☐ Box braids   ☐ Crown braid

I wonder:

244

Date: /   /

Location: _____

KALEIDOSCOPE

☐ Paper   ☐ Metal   ☐ Wooden

I wonder:

245

Date: /   /

Location: _____

BARBER'S POLE

☐ Rotating   ☐ Red and white   ☐ Red, white, and blue

I wonder:

246

Date: /   /

Location: _____

FRUIT SKIN

☐ Pineapple   ☐ Asian pear   ☐ Cherimoya

I wonder:

LAG

Date: / /

Location: _____

☐ Pride ☐ For semaphore signaling ☐ Meaningful to you

wonder:

EWER COVER

Date: / /

Location: _____

☐ Has letters ☐ Has pictures ☐ Emitting steam

wonder:

ARBLEIZED PAPER

Date: / /

Location: _____

☐ At paper shop ☐ Book endpaper ☐ Video of making it

wonder:

QUILT

Date: / /

Location: _____

☐ "Flying geese" ☐ "Churn dash" ☐ Improvisational

wonder:

SPECIAL OCCASION

I've noticed something: When special occasions are approaching, people start making things. They make *extra special* things. Food. Clothing. Decorations. Gifts. Music. Plans. Invitations. I believe every moment of every day is special. And yet, some moments and some days are extra special. On a regular day, I might fry an egg at home for breakfast. On an extra special day, such as my birthday, I might go to my favorite brunch spot and order eggs Benedict with hollandaise sauce. Sometimes it's good to push pause and say: *Wow! This is important! Let's celebrate!*

One way we can mark a moment as important is to make it beautiful. When I was a kid, I loved to stop and peek through the window at my local bakery. They kept a milk crate out on the sidewalk so that kids like me could climb up and get a better view of the birthday cakes being decorated. I was mesmerized as I watched colored icing ooze out of the little metal tip of the pastry bag into all sorts of fancy shapes: yellow rose swirls, textured green leaves, delicate blue latticework, fancy cursive letters. I could have watched for hours and hours. In fact, I liked watching cakes be decorated even more than eating them!

WHO ELSE IS EATING A MOONCAKE AT THE SAME EXACT MOMENT AS ME?

• • •

WHY HAVE I SEEN MORE LUNAR ECLIPSES THAN SOLAR ECLIPSES?

• • •

I WONDER HOW MANY DIFFERENT SPECIAL WAYS I CAN FOLD THIS NAPKIN.

SPECIAL OCCASION

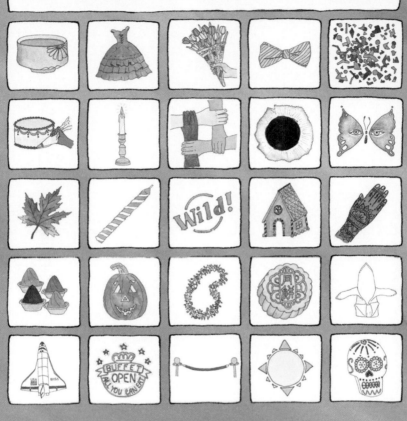

Object:

Date: /   /

Location: _____

I wonder:

252

Date: /   /

Location: _____

☐ Being applied   ☐ On groom   ☐ On bride

HENNA

I wonder:

253

Date: /   /

Location: _____

☐ In India   ☐ In Nepal   ☐ In your town

HOLI

I wonder:

254

Date: /   /

Location: _____

☐ On altar   ☐ Edible   ☐ Decorated by you

SUGAR SKULL

I wonder:

255

Date: /   /

Location: _____

☐ Lotus seed filling   ☐ Red bean   ☐ Egg yolk

MOONCAKE

I wonder:

INGERBREAD HOUSE

Date: / /

Location: _____

☐ Elaborate   ☐ Made by you   ☐ Eaten by you

wonder:

IRST BIRTHDAY

Date: / /

Location: _____

☐ Cake   ☐ Smiling   ☐ Crying

wonder:

EI

Date: / /

Location: _____

☐ Orchids   ☐ Plumerias   ☐ Carnations

wonder:

ONFETTI

Date: / /

Location: _____

☐ Paper   ☐ Homemade   ☐ Rainbow colored

wonder:

260

Date: / /

Location: _____

☐ Striped ☐ Polka dotted ☐ Silk

BOW TIE

I wonder:

261

Date: / /

Location: _____

☐ At restaurant ☐ At home ☐ Cloth

FANCY FOLDED NAPKIN

I wonder:

262

Date: / /

Location: _____

☐ Dinnertime ☐ On a cake ☐ Power outage

CANDLELIGHT

I wonder:

263

Date: / /

Location: _____

☐ Butterfly ☐ Animal ☐ At sports game

FACE PAINTING

I wonder:

UMMER SOLSTICE

Date: /   /

Location: _____

☐ Watched sunrise   ☐ Played in sunshine   ☐ Parade

wonder:

EA CEREMONY

Date: /   /

Location: _____

☐ Tea room   ☐ Tatami mats   ☐ Chasen

wonder:

ALL COLORS

Date: /   /

Location: _____

☐ Maple leaf   ☐ Oak leaf   ☐ Many trees together

wonder:

CLIPSE

Date: /   /

Location: _____

☐ Lunar   ☐ Solar   ☐ Total

wonder:

268

Date: / /

CAKE DECORATING

Location: _____

☐ Bakery window ☐ At home ☐ Icing flowers

I wonder

269

Date: / /

DANCING AT A PARTY

Location: _____

☐ Right-hand star ☐ DJ ☐ Live band

I wonder

270

Date: / /

SPECIAL RESTAURANT

Location: _____

☐ Favorite ☐ First time ☐ Long line

I wonder

271

Date: / /

VELVET ROPE

Location: _____

☐ Work of art ☐ Historical artifact ☐ Movie premiere

I wonder

~~P~~OOFY DRESS

Date: /   /

Location: _____

☐ Quinceañera   ☐ Drag   ☐ Award ceremony

wonder:

~~J~~ACK-O-LANTERN

Date: /   /

Location: _____

☐ Scary   ☐ Friendly   ☐ Carved by you

wonder:

~~S~~PACECRAFT LAUNCH

Date: /   /

Location: _____

☐ On TV   ☐ In person   ☐ In newspaper

wonder:

~~B~~OUQUET OF FLOWERS

Date: /   /

Location: _____

☐ For you   ☐ From you   ☐ In stranger's hand

wonder:

FROM HERE TO THERE

Between "here" and "there" isn't just empty *space*, but an interesting *place*. On an airplane, I try to get the window seat so I can enjoy a bird's-eye view of the changing landscape. In the car, I like to decipher license plates and sing along to my favorite songs. On foot, I keep an eye out for beautiful blossoms, free fruit, and friends.

There is a tiny creature I admire who reminds me to make the distance between point A and point B a delight: a leafcutter ant. It has been my favorite animal ever since I crossed paths with a whole caravan of them in the rain forest in Costa Rica. Petite yet powerful, leafcutter ants carefully cut and collect segments of leaves to carry back to their nest. They look very busy and are clearly working hard, but it also looks like fun. It is a tiny parade! Sometimes there are even pink petals mixed in with the bright green bits. This little celebration takes place every day with no special occasion required. I try to follow the ants' lead. Whenever I am on a trip—however big or small—I keep my eyes open for something to celebrate along the way.

WHY IS THIS ROUTE "HISTORIC"? WHO USED TO TRAVEL ALONG IT MANY YEARS BEFORE ME?

• • •

CAN I GET A PAPER MAP OF MY TOWN AND HIGHLIGHT EVERYWHERE I'VE BEEN?

• • •

A POSTAGE STAMP IS LIKE A TINY PLANE TICKET FOR AN ENVELOPE!

FROM HERE TO THERE

Object:

Date: / /

Location: _____

wonder:

Wild!

277

Date: /   /

LOST LUGGAGE

Location: _____

☐ Suitcase   ☐ Duffel   ☐ Very upsetting

I wonder:

278

Date: /   /

DIRT ROAD

Location: _____

☐ On foot   ☐ On bicycle   ☐ In car

I wonder:

279

Date: /   /

BOAT RIDE

Location: _____

☐ Sailboat   ☐ Ferry   ☐ Seasick

I wonder:

280

Date: /   /

TRAVEL SNACKS

Location: _____

☐ Pretzels   ☐ Chips   ☐ Dried fruit

I wonder:

SOMEONE MOVING

Date: / /

Location: _____

□ Best friend □ Neighbor □ You

wonder:

HISTORIC ROAD

Date: / /

Location: _____

□ Official sign □ On vacation □ Scenic

wonder:

SHARING AN
UMBRELLA

Date: / /

Location: _____

□ Yellow □ Curved handle □ With two or more friends

wonder:

PAPER MAP

Date: / /

Location: _____

□ Folded neatly □ In glove compartment □ Hand-drawn

wonder:

285

Date: /   /

Location: _____

THE WINDOW SEAT

☐ Ocean view   ☐ Mountain view   ☐ At sunset

I wonder:

286

Date: /   /

Location: _____

PASSPORT

☐ Lots of stamps   ☐ Humorous photo   ☐ Expired

I wonder:

287

Date: /   /

Location: _____

GETTING LOST

☐ In car   ☐ On purpose   ☐ Also running late

I wonder:

288

Date: /   /

Location: _____

LICENSE PLATE FROM FAR AWAY

☐ Out of state   ☐ Out of country   ☐ Out of continent

I wonder:

LA R 2324

PEDICAB

Date: /   /

Location: _____

☐ Two-seater   ☐ Four-seater   ☐ Friendly driver

wonder:

PRESSED PENNY

Date: /   /

Location: _____

☐ Zoo   ☐ Aquarium   ☐ Lighthouse

wonder:

GOING THROUGH
A TUNNEL

Date: /   /

Location: _____

☐ Covered bridge   ☐ Underground   ☐ Held your breath

wonder:

ROADSIDE FARM STAND

Date: /   /

Location: _____

☐ Pumpkins   ☐ Flowers   ☐ Honor system

wonder:

HONOR SYSTEM
PAY HERE

293

Date: / /

Location: _____

☐ Passenger ☐ Cargo ☐ Steam-powered

TRAIN

I wonder:

294

Date: / /

Location: _____

☐ Kid inside ☐ Carrying plants ☐ Classic red

PULL WAGON

I wonder:

295

Date: / /

Location: _____

☐ Plant bits ☐ Other ants ☐ Mystery items

ANTS CARRYING THINGS

I wonder:

296

Date: / /

Location: _____

☐ Round trip ☐ Extra long ☐ Sore feet

A LONG WALK

I wonder:

OSTAGE STAMP

Date: /   /

Location: _____

☐ Postcard-rate   ☐ Historical figure   ☐ Lick-and-stick type

wonder:

PECIAL SHOES

Date: /   /

Location: _____

☐ Snowshoes   ☐ Steel-toed boots   ☐ Bunny slippers

wonder:

ALKING MAZE

Date: /   /

Location: _____

☐ Corn maze   ☐ Hedge maze   ☐ Labyrinth

wonder:

ANE

Date: /   /

Location: _____

☐ Duck head handle   ☐ For blind   ☐ Quad

wonder:

HANDWORK

I have loved working with my hands since I was a wee one forming clay into a pinch pot. I vividly remember learning to shuffle a deck of playing cards with the "bridge" technique when I was about ten, practicing again and again until I could do it. Back then, my dad worked in downtown Los Angeles near Little Tokyo, so occasionally I got to go to the stationery store there, spending my savings on packs of origami paper.

Mountain fold. Valley fold. Crease, pinch, turn, tuck! Origami was magic. Just follow the step-by-step diagram, and a simple square of paper turned into a tiny crane or frog, bear or balloon. Right before my eyes, two dimensions shapeshifted into 3-D. Practically nothing suddenly became something! From one book, I learned to fold elaborate, hexagonal boxes with lids. From another, I memorized how to fold a dollar bill into a finger ring.

These days, as a grown-up, the jumping frog is my favorite to fold. I keep origami paper in an old mint tin in my purse, so I am always ready. The fold that completes it creates a spot for a fingertip on the frog's back. Press down and release, and the little paper pal goes: HOP!

I WONDER WHAT INSPIRED THE PARTICULAR PATTERN WOVEN INTO THAT BASKET.

• • •

DO DRUMMERS' HANDS GET SORE BY THE END OF A LONG CONCERT?

• • •

A RASPBERRY IS A VERY CONVENIENT SIZE FOR MY FINGERTIPS TO GRASP.

HANDWORK

Object:

Date: /   /

Location: _____

I wonder:

Wild!

302

Date: ___ / ___ / ___
Location: _____

INDIGENOUS BEADWORK

☐ Ojibwe   ☐ Haudenosaunee   ☐ Huichol

I wonder:

303

Date: ___ / ___ / ___
Location: _____

"BRIDGE" SHUFFLE TECHNIQUE

☐ Expert   ☐ Learning how   ☐ Big mess

I wonder:

304

Date: ___ / ___ / ___
Location: _____

HAND-WOVEN BASKET

☐ Nimiipuu berry   ☐ Mushrooming   ☐ Easter

I wonder:

305

Date: ___ / ___ / ___
Location: _____

PINCUSHION

☐ Multi-colored pins   ☐ Tomato shape   ☐ Hand-me-down

I wonder:

NJERA

Date: /   /

Location: _____

☐ Freshly made   ☐ Spongey   ☐ Beautifully spiraled

wonder:

HANDMADE VALENTINE

Date: /   /

Location: _____

☐ Given   ☐ For a friend   ☐ From a secret admirer

wonder:

GLASSWORK

Date: /   /

Location: _____

☐ Figurine being formed   ☐ Furnace   ☐ Glowing red glass

wonder:

ORIGAMI

Date: /   /

Location: _____

☐ Animal   ☐ From memory   ☐ One thousand cranes

wonder:

310

Date: / /

Location: _____

COOKIE FRESH FROM OVEN

☐ Still warm   ☐ Favorite kind   ☐ Good scent

I wonder:

311

Date: / /

Location: _____

DJEMBE

☐ Carved wood   ☐ Drum circle   ☐ Good beat

I wonder:

312

Date: / /

Location: _____

HAND-KNIT GARMENT

☐ Hat   ☐ Sweater   ☐ Socks

I wonder:

313

Date: / /

Location: _____

PATCHED CLOTHING

☐ Elbow   ☐ Knee   ☐ Yours

I wonder:

HOE REPAIR SHOP

Date: /   /

Location: _____

☐ Scent of glue   ☐ Giant shoe sign   ☐ Large shoelace selection

wonder:

314

HITTLING

Date: /   /

Location: _____

☐ Bear   ☐ Bird   ☐ Toy

wonder:

315

IGN LANGUAGE

Date: /   /

Location: _____

☐ "I love you"   ☐ Conversation   ☐ Interpreter

wonder:

316

OMEONE PAINTING N PUBLIC

Date: /   /

Location: _____

☐ Watercolor   ☐ Oil paint   ☐ Mural

wonder:

317

318

Date: /   /

Location: _____

☐ On envelope   ☐ Invitation   ☐ Written by you

YOUR NAME IN CALLIGRAPHY

I wonder:

319

Date: /   /

Location: _____

☐ Rope   ☐ Pretzel   ☐ Hairdo

FANCY KNOT

I wonder:

320

Date: /   /

Location: _____

☐ Raspberry   ☐ Garden   ☐ U-pick farm

BERRY PICKED BY YOU

I wonder:

321

Date: /   /

Location: _____

☐ To you   ☐ From you   ☐ Feeling loved

CARE PACKAGE

I wonder:

HANDMADE TORTILLAS

Date: /   /

Location: _____

☐ Corn   ☐ Flour   ☐ Tortilla press

wonder:

HANDMADE BIRD HOUSE

Date: /   /

Location: _____

☐ Wooden   ☐ Occupied   ☐ Made with hand tools

wonder:

PLUCKING POMEGRANATE SEEDS

Date: /   /

Location: _____

☐ Bright red   ☐ Splattered shirt   ☐ Some rotten

wonder:

SPLIT KINDLING

Date: /   /

Location: _____

☐ Thin   ☐ Bundled   ☐ Fresh scent

wonder:

HOME SWEET HOME

One time while hiking, I spotted a beautiful shell on the trail. I picked it up, thinking I might take it home with me. But as I turned the elegant spiral over in my palm to admire it from all angles, I quickly realized that it was not for the taking. "It" was actually a "who." Someone—a very small gooey creature—was inside. Oops! I had accidentally collected someone's home. I quickly put the snail back where I had found it. "Sorry, friend!" As I did so, it occurred to me that I might have been the reason the snail's body was squeezed so deep inside their shell. Were they scared? Hiding from me? Just napping?

Homes are special spaces no matter what their design: small, big, old, new, colorful, on wheels, for people or for other creatures. Snails get one home; they grow it themselves and take it with them wherever they go. Human homes tend to come and go over time. We build them for each other and share them with future generations. Whenever it is time for me to move into a new home, I visit my old home one last time and say thank you to each empty room, as if it were a beautiful old shell.

HOW DOES AN IGLOO KEEP PEOPLE WARM IF IT IS MADE OF SNOW?

•••

IF I HAD A DOLLHOUSE, I WOULD CRAFT MY OWN TINY BOOKS FOR IT, WITH REAL PAGES.

•••

I WONDER IF BIRDS REUSE THEIR NESTS OR BUILD NEW ONES EACH YEAR.

home sweet home

Object:

Date: /   /

Location: _____

I wonder:

Wild!

327

Date: /   /

VICTORIAN PORCH

Location: _____

☐ Bright colors   ☐ Spent time on   ☐ "Gingerbread" woodwork

I wonder:

328

Date: /   /

COMFORT FOOD

Location: _____

☐ Mac 'n' cheese   ☐ Soup   ☐ Herb tea

I wonder:

329

Date: /   /

SHELL

Location: _____

☐ Empty   ☐ Patterned   ☐ Living creature inside

I wonder:

330

Date: /   /

DOLLHOUSE

Location: _____

☐ Tiny books   ☐ Made with Legos   ☐ Belongs to a grown-up

I wonder:

PRESIDENT'S HOUSE

Date: /   /

Location: _____

☐ In person   ☐ On TV   ☐ In newspaper

wonder:

WOODSTOVE

Date: /   /

Location: _____

☐ Iron   ☐ Glowing   ☐ Cozy

wonder:

BIRD NEST

Date: /   /

Location: _____

☐ With eggs   ☐ Empty   ☐ Too high to know

wonder:

IGLOO

Date: /   /

Location: _____

☐ In person   ☐ In a book   ☐ Video of construction

wonder:

335

Date: / /

DOORMAT

Location: _____

☐ "Welcome" ☐ Natural material ☐ Recycled plastic

I wonder:

WELCOME

336

Date: / /

AQUARIUM

Location: _____

☐ In a home ☐ Bioluminescence ☐ Touch tank

I wonder:

337

Date: / /

PRAYER FLAGS

Location: _____

☐ At temple ☐ On porch ☐ Faded and wind worn

I wonder:

338

Date: / /

SIDEWALK ART

Location: _____

☐ By you ☐ In your neighborhood ☐ At festival

I wonder:

12

CHALK
12

CHICKEN COOP

Date: / /

Location: _____

☐ Rhode Island Red   ☐ Cochin   ☐ Rooster present

wonder:

WASP NEST

Date: / /

Location: _____

☐ In roof   ☐ Stung   ☐ No longer in use

wonder:

HOME BEING PAINTED

Date: / /

Location: _____

☐ New color   ☐ Scaffolding   ☐ Contrasting window trim

wonder:

EXTERIOR
SEMI
GLOSS

A MEMORABLE DREAM

Date: / /

Location: _____

☐ Magical   ☐ Unpleasant   ☐ Told someone about it

wonder:

DREAMS

343 MOBILE HOME

Date: /   /

Location: _____

☐ Canned-ham style ☐ Tear-drop ☐ Mobile home community

I wonder:

344 MEZUZAH

Date: /   /

Location: _____

☐ Leaning left ☐ Inscribed design ☐ At your doorway

I wonder:

345 HOME RUN

Date: /   /

Location: _____

☐ Out of the park ☐ Grand slam ☐ Slid home

I wonder:

346 WINDOW BOX GARDEN

Date: /   /

Location: _____

☐ Succulents ☐ Tomatoes ☐ Herbs

I wonder:

EMPORARY DIGS

Date: /   /

Location: _____

☐ Hotel   ☐ With family   ☐ With friends

wonder:

EARTHEN BUILDING

Date: /   /

Location: _____

☐ Adobe   ☐ Cob   ☐ Straw bale

wonder:

TENT

Date: /   /

Location: _____

☐ Camping   ☐ In town   ☐ Zipper windows

wonder:

HOUSE KEY

Date: /   /

Location: _____

☐ Your own   ☐ Fun keychain   ☐ Lost!

wonder:

EVERYTHING COUNTS

I have a rule for myself. If I come across a hopscotch course, I must hop it. Short or long, colorful or plain, I jump into the first square and go from there! I am a connoisseur of hopscotch. I like to notice the different design strategies and difficulty levels. One time, I encountered one with more than one route—halfway through, it forked into two paths and then came back together, like a river flowing around an island. Another time, I found a hopscotch course in the shape of a big blue heart. The numbered boxes filled the inside of the heart. It required some fancy footwork to complete it as the numbers were not in order. Some of the squares were so small that only the toe of my shoe would fit!

I like to dream up new hopscotch designs. One time, I made a surprise hopscotch course for a friend, putting the #1 square at their doorstep so they would see it when they left their house. Someday, I'd like to draw one at a bus stop so people can hop it and then keep hopping right onto the bus. Another idea: an infinity hopscotch that goes around my entire block!

IN OTHER LANGUAGES, DOES THE WORD FOR "INCHWORM" REFERENCE ITS SIZE ON A RULER?

• • •

I WONDER HOW MANY TEASPOONS ARE IN A TABLESPOON.

• • •

HOW OFTEN DO THEY PUT A NEW ROLL OF NUMBERS IN THE "TAKE-A-NUMBER" DISPENSER?

EVERYTHING COUNTS

Object:

Date: / /

Location: _____

I wonder:

Wild!

352

Date: / /

A VERY LONG RECEIPT

Location: _____

☐ At grocery ☐ At post office ☐ Lots of coupons

I wonder:

353

Date: / /

A TRIO

Location: _____

☐ Ice cream ☐ Music band ☐ Triplets

I wonder:

354

Date: / /

SUDOKU GAME IN PROGRESS

Location: _____

☐ At home ☐ Stranger ☐ On bus

I wonder:

355

Date: / /

A PIE CHART

Location: _____

☐ Interesting ☐ Boring ☐ Confusing

I wonder:

NCHWORM

Date: /   /

Location: _____

☐ On stem   ☐ On your fingertip   ☐ Dangling from plant

wonder:

PRECISE
EASUREMENT

Date: /   /

Location: _____

☐ In inches   ☐ In centimeters   ☐ Bigger than you

wonder:

XTRA-LONG
IOPSCOTCH COURSE

Date: /   /

Location: _____

☐ Over 10 squares   ☐ Over 100   ☐ Hopped it

wonder:

IE WITH MORE
HAN SIX SIDES

Date: /   /

Location: _____

☐ Octahedron (8)   ☐ Dodecahedron (12)   ☐ Icosahedron (20)

wonder:

360

Date: / /

Location: _____

COMBO LOCK

☐ On locker ☐ On diary ☐ Forgotten code

I wonder:

361

Date: / /

Location: _____

A VERY LONG LINE

☐ Number dispenser ☐ Impatient people ☐ Worth the wait

I wonder:

362

Date: / /

Location: _____

FRUIT SLICED INTO EIGHTHS

☐ Orange ☐ Apple ☐ Kiwi

I wonder:

363

Date: / /

Location: _____

NUMBER ON FINGERS

☐ A child's age ☐ The number 3 ☐ Using both hands

I wonder:

FASCINATING STATISTIC

Date: / /

Location: _____

☐ A percentage   ☐ A diagram   ☐ Told at the dinner table

wonder:

%

364

CALCULATOR WATCH

Date: / /

Location: _____

☐ 20th century   ☐ Tiny buttons   ☐ Functioning

wonder:

365

ROTARY TELEPHONE

Date: / /

Location: _____

☐ Heard a dial tone   ☐ Dialed it   ☐ In thrift store

wonder:

366

ABACUS

Date: / /

Location: _____

☐ Wooden beads   ☐ Learned to use it   ☐ Ancient specimen

wonder:

367

368

Date: /   /

Location: _____

☐ Simple picture   ☐ Elaborate picture   ☐ Made a mistake

I wonder:

369

Date: /   /

Location: _____

☐ Pencil   ☐ Marker   ☐ Yours

DOORWAY HEIGHT GROWTH CHART

I wonder:

Amy
7.2.84

Amy
12.11.93

3.6.82 Amy

Sarah
7.2.84

370

Date: /   /

Location: _____

☐ White pips   ☐ Dragons on back   ☐ Falling show

DOMINOES

I wonder:

371

Date: /   /

Location: _____

☐ Involving dates   ☐ Involving money   ☐ Impressive

MENTAL MATH

I wonder:

MEASURING SPOONS

Date: / /

Location: _____

□ Oval   □ Circular   □ Set of six

wonder:

STAMP CANCELLATION MARK

Date: / /

Location: _____

□ Important date   □ Your birthdate   □ A long time ago

wonder:

TWINS

Date: / /

Location: _____

□ Surprise   □ Identical   □ Fraternal

wonder:

HALF & HALF

Date: / /

Location: _____

□ Small carton   □ Single-serve cup   □ Cow image on carton

wonder:

BODIES IN MOTION

Everything is on the move. This is because Earth itself never stops. Not only is it spinning on its axis like a ballet dancer, but the Earth is also orbiting the Sun at 67,000 mph. Wow! In other words, in every moment, our bodies—mine, yours, a squirrel's, a succulent's—are hurtling through outer space at an incredibly high speed. Even when you're cozy in bed, you are soaring. Isn't that weird and wonderful? I therefore consider myself an astronaut. My mission is to explore the surface of this weird and wonderful planet Earth as it dances through space.

Won't you join me? We can study sidewalks on roller skates and research snow from a sled. From a roller coaster, we can get to know gravity, then grab our oars and search for signs of water. From up in a hot-air balloon, we can draw maps and document the land-form patterns below. We can record the flight paths of butterflies, measure the length of snail trail dashes, and count the dust bunnies hiding in the corners of our dining rooms. Every new discovery can inspire a celebratory jig—a happy dance to celebrate this little nook of the universe we call home.

WHY DO BODIES SWEAT WHEN THEY ARE PHYSICALLY ACTIVE?

• • •

BUTTERFLIES LOOK LIKE THEY'RE DANCING.

• • •

WHALES DON'T NEED PASSPORTS AND CAN CROSS NATIONAL BOUNDARIES AS THEY WISH.

BODIES IN MOTION

Object:

Date: / /

Location: _____

wonder:

Wild!

377

Date: /   /

Location: _____

☐ Under your feet   ☐ Right now   ☐ Always

PLANET EARTH

I wonder

378

Date: /   /

Location: _____

☐ Flamenco   ☐ Musical theater   ☐ Friend performing

A DANCE PERFORMANCE

I wonder

379

Date: /   /

Location: _____

☐ Stripes   ☐ Zig-zags   ☐ Festival

HOT-AIR BALLOON

I wonder

380

Date: /   /

Location: _____

☐ Fundraiser   ☐ Olympics   ☐ Participated

A RUNNING RACE

I wonder

3192
RUN
for
BREAST
CANCER

OCCER GAME

Date: / /

Location: _____

□ Park □ On TV □ Oranges at half time

wonder:

381

LEVATOR RIDE

Date: / /

Location: _____

□ Glass walls □ Great view □ 13th floor

wonder:

382

OMEONE ROWING

Date: / /

Location: _____

□ Rowboat □ Canoe □ Kayak

wonder:

383

LED RIDE

Date: / /

Location: _____

□ Snow □ Sand dunes □ Too fast but fun

wonder:

384

385

Date: / /

Location: _____

ROCK CLIMBING WALL

☐ Colorful ropes   ☐ Fun to watch   ☐ You climbed it

I wonder:

386

Date: / /

Location: _____

WEIGHT LIFTING

☐ 5 lbs.   ☐ Heavy backpack   ☐ Lots of groceries

I wonder:

387

Date: / /

Location: _____

CAROUSEL RIDE

☐ Horse   ☐ Zebra   ☐ Unicorn

I wonder:

388

Date: / /

Location: _____

PROSTHETIC

☐ Family   ☐ Friend   ☐ Paralympic athlete

I wonder:

UMBLEWEED

Date: / /

Location: _____

☐ In motion ☐ Across road ☐ Huge

wonder:

ATELLITE IN SKY

Date: / /

Location: _____

☐ Moving fast ☐ Mistook for star ☐ Watched until out of sight

wonder:

ROLLER SKATING

Date: / /

Location: _____

☐ At park ☐ At roller rink ☐ Fancy footwork

wonder:

NAIL TRAIL

Date: / /

Location: _____

☐ Dashed line ☐ On sidewalk ☐ On plant

wonder:

393

Date: / /

BARF BAG

Location: _____

☐ Unused ☐ Had to use ☐ Almost had to use

I wonder:

MOTION DISCOMFORT BAG

394

Date: / /

LEARNING TO DANCE

Location: _____

☐ Waltz ☐ Online video ☐ Salsa

I wonder:

395

Date: / /

ROLLER COASTER RIDE

Location: _____

☐ Fun! ☐ Scary! ☐ Nauseating!

I wonder:

396

Date: / /

MIGRATING ANIMAL

Location: _____

☐ Monarch butterfly ☐ Canada goose ☐ Whale

I wonder:

UST BUNNIES

Date: / /

Location: _____

☐ Left them be   ☐ Swept them up   ☐ Hiding in corner

wonder:

BATON TWIRLING

Date: / /

Location: _____

☐ Parade   ☐ Half-time show   ☐ Lesson

wonder:

ANDEM BICYCLE

Date: / /

Location: _____

☐ Cruiser handlebar   ☐ Basket   ☐ Saddle bags

wonder:

BIRDS FLYING IN V FORMATION

Date: / /

Location: _____

☐ Flying north   ☐ Flying south   ☐ Lead bird swap

wonder:

BIG THINGS

The magnitude, or size, of a thing is not meaningful unless we have something else to compare it to. I am a giant compared to an ant, but I feel quite small looking up the trunk of a giant redwood tree. A strawberry is only "huge" compared to the size of our mouths and the rest of the strawberries we have ever seen. That same berry is no longer huge when held up against the night sky. It's all relative!

The word "big," though, is not only for physical dimensions. It can also refer to importance or big emotions. A volcano or a whale is obviously big, but so are acts of courage like learning to swim or making a new friend. In the grand scheme of things, it might not seem like a big deal, but it is if it's happening to you!

I remember when I was a child, I was nervous when I flew on an airplane for the first time without my parents. They filled my carry-on bag with treats to comfort me and give me courage: a book to read, a sketch pad and colored pencils, a brand-new package of our family's favorite cookies. I read, colored, and nibbled all the way to Cincinnati, where my aunt greeted me with a big hug!

WHY DOESN'T THIS SUPER-TALL SUNFLOWER FALL OVER?

• • •

I WONDER HOW GEOGRAPHICALLY LARGE THE POWER OUTAGE IS.

• • •

THE OCEAN IS HUGE, BUT IT IS MADE OF TINY THINGS: MANY DROPS OF WATER!

BIG THINGS

Object:

Date: /   /

Location: _____

I wonder:

Wild!

402

Date: / /

Location: _____

TEARS

☐ Of joy ☐ Of sadness ☐ Of frustration

I wonder:

403

Date: / /

Location: _____

IFTAR MEAL

☐ Three dates ☐ Eid al-Fitr ☐ Public gathering

I wonder:

404

Date: / /

Location: _____

HUGE STRAWBERRY

☐ One bite ☐ Many bites ☐ More than 300 seeds

I wonder:

405

Date: / /

Location: _____

VIEW THROUGH A TELESCOPE

☐ Constellation ☐ Moon ☐ Another planet

I wonder:

PLANETARIUM SHOW

Date: /   /

Location: _____

☐ Loved it   ☐ Fell asleep   ☐ Ticket stub souvenir

wonder:

STRONG WIND

Date: /   /

Location: _____

☐ Whistling sound   ☐ Windswept hair   ☐ Difficult to walk in

wonder:

THUNDER AND LIGHTNING

Date: /   /

Location: _____

☐ Woke you up   ☐ Calculated distance   ☐ Nearby

wonder:

VERY BIG WAVE

Date: /   /

Location: _____

☐ Boat ride   ☐ While swimming   ☐ Someone surfed it

wonder:

410

Date: / /

Location: _____

VOLCANO

☐ Active ☐ Inactive ☐ Currently an island

I wonder:

411

Date: / /

Location: _____

FIRST DAY OF SCHOOL

☐ Cool book bag ☐ Good lunch ☐ Kind teacher

I wonder:

412

Date: / /

Location: _____

POWER OUTAGE

☐ Used flashlights ☐ Used candles ☐ Daytime

I wonder:

413

Date: / /

Location: _____

A RIVER

☐ Wide ☐ Meandering ☐ Swam in it

I wonder:

CEMENT TRUCK

Date: / /

Location: _____

☐ Rotating while driving　☐ Pouring cement　☐ Long chute

wonder:

LEARNING TO SWIM

Date: / /

Location: _____

☐ Pool　☐ River　☐ Ocean

wonder:

A MOMENT OF COURAGE

Date: / /

Location: _____

☐ Tried something new　☐ Felt emotion　☐ Glad you did it

wonder:

NEWBORN BABY

Date: / /

Location: _____

☐ Sibling　☐ Cousin　☐ On day of birth

wonder:

418

Date: / /

Location: _____

MYCORRHIZAL NETWORK

☐ Saw it ☐ Thought about it ☐ Learned about it

I wonder:

419

Date: / /

Location: _____

SUNFLOWER TALLER THAN YOU

☐ Barely taller ☐ Much taller ☐ Full of seeds

I wonder:

420

Date: / /

Location: _____

DRAGON DANCE

☐ More than 15 dancers ☐ More than 46 ☐ Double dragon

I wonder:

421

Date: / /

Location: _____

OVERHEARD: "I DO"

☐ With tears ☐ With smiles ☐ With laughter

I wonder:

DINOSAUR SKELETON

Date: / /

Location: _____

☐ Triceratops ☐ Brontosaurus ☐ Tyrannosaurus rex

wonder:

THE FUTURE

Date: / /

Location: _____

☐ Eager for ☐ Anxious about ☐ Curious about

wonder:

SKY WRITING

Date: / /

Location: _____

☐ Birthday wish ☐ Advertisement ☐ Marriage proposal

wonder:

A WHALE

Date: / /

Location: _____

☐ From boat ☐ Through binoculars ☐ Listened to songs

wonder:

SCENTS & SOUNDS

I love the scent of roses, lavender, and a walk in a redwood forest. I would rather peel a tangerine than slice one so I can enjoy the scent that sprays out of the skin as I tear the peel off. Tangerines remind me of my friend Akira. The smallest whiff of tuberose perfume sparks good memories of my grandmother.

On its own, asphalt doesn't really catch my attention or bring me joy. It is just sort of there, in the background. But all that changes when it begins to rain. Oh, I love that scent! Even the scent, though, isn't particularly delicious or good on its own. What's good is the memory it stirs up. It makes me happy because it instantly transports me back to the rainy days of elementary school. Lunchtime would take place inside the classroom while the rain poured down on the four-square courts outside. Some of my classmates itched to play outdoors, but I preferred to be in class with the art supplies. So the scent of rain on asphalt meant that after I finished my PB&J, I could do art at my desk. Rainy day meant art day! These days, though I'm grown up, it still does.

WHY IS IT SO DIFFICULT TO DESCRIBE SCENTS WITH WORDS?

• • •

I WONDER WHAT MY HEARTBEAT SOUNDS LIKE THROUGH MY DOCTOR'S STETHOSCOPE.

• • •

THE SOUND OF THAT CREEK IS CALMING.

Scents & Sounds

Object:

I wonder:

Date: /   /

Location: _____

427

Date: / /

Location: _____

FRAGRANT FLOWERS

☐ Lily   ☐ Honeysuckle   ☐ Jasmine

I wonder:

428

Date: / /

Location: _____

POTPOURRI

☐ Flowers   ☐ Seeds   ☐ Wood shavings

I wonder:

429

Date: / /

Location: _____

SKUNK

☐ Scent only   ☐ Saw it   ☐ Roadkill

I wonder:

430

Date: / /

Location: _____

SALMON

☐ Fish market   ☐ Smoked   ☐ Caught by someone you know

I wonder:

BAR OF SOAP

Date: ___ / ___ / ___

Location: _____

☐ Floral   ☐ Fruity   ☐ Unscented

wonder:

431

DOG DOO

Date: ___ / ___ / ___

Location: _____

☐ On your shoe   ☐ Smelled it first   ☐ Being picked up

wonder:

432

ROTTING FRUIT

Date: ___ / ___ / ___

Location: _____

☐ On counter   ☐ On sidewalk   ☐ On tree

wonder:

433

RAIN ON ASPHALT

Date: ___ / ___ / ___

Location: _____

☐ Enjoyable   ☐ Unpleasant   ☐ Reminds you of . . .

wonder:

434

435

Date: / /

Location: _____

CITRUS PEEL SPRAY

☐ Tangerine ☐ Lime ☐ Grapefruit

I wonder:

436

Date: / /

Location: _____

LAVENDER

☐ Dried flowers ☐ Flavoring ☐ Plant growing

I wonder:

437

Date: / /

Location: _____

PERFUME

☐ Delightful ☐ Too strong ☐ Antique bottle

I wonder:

438

Date: / /

Location: _____

FRESH GINGER

☐ Stir-fry ☐ Curry ☐ Gingerbread

I wonder:

SURPRISING INSTRUMENT

Date: /   /

Location: _____

☐ The spoons   ☐ Armpit   ☐ Makeshift drum

wonder:

TEA KETTLE

Date: /   /

Location: _____

☐ Whistle   ☐ Click   ☐ Sounds like a train

wonder:

HEARTBEAT

Date: /   /

Location: _____

☐ Yours   ☐ Parent's   ☐ Pet's

wonder:

CAPOEIRA TOQUES

Date: /   /

Location: _____

☐ Hand claps   ☐ Berimbaus   ☐ Singing

wonder:

443

Date: / /

ORGAN MUSIC

Location: _____

☐ In theater   ☐ At ballpark   ☐ At church

I wonder:

444

Date: / /

FROGS CROAKING

Location: _____

☐ Morning   ☐ Midday   ☐ Evening

I wonder:

445

Date: / /

BEES BUZZING

Location: _____

☐ Honeybee boxes   ☐ In garden   ☐ Hiding in flowers

I wonder:

446

Date: / /

WIND CHIMES

Location: _____

☐ Wooden   ☐ Shells   ☐ Colorful

I wonder:

ICADA CHORUS

Date: /   /

Location: _____

☐ Piercing   ☐ Pulsating   ☐ Droning

wonder:

ANGUAGE YOU DON'T
KNOW

Date: /   /

Location: _____

☐ In person   ☐ In your home   ☐ In video

wonder:

ARMONY

Date: /   /

Location: _____

☐ A cappella   ☐ Choir   ☐ Beautiful

wonder:

RUNNING WATER

Date: /   /

Location: _____

☐ Fountain   ☐ Creek   ☐ Waterfall

wonder:

THESE THINGS TAKE TIME

Do you remember learning to write? In kindergarten, they introduced each letter of the alphabet to us with a song and an inflatable toy in the shape of an "A," "B," or other letter. In third grade, I learned cursive—a script font with linked letters and lots of loops. I loved to draw, so the homework was fun. With a pencil, I copied the shapes of the letters again and again until I knew each one by heart.

There are other scripts that I know by heart: the handwriting of my loved ones. I have recipes in my grandmother's beautiful, slanted cursive. I save birthday cards with my grandfather's unique spin on architectural lettering—all caps, with a surprising little loop tossed in here and there. I would recognize my parents' handwriting anywhere, from the slow, careful lettering of heartfelt notes to the quick, looser versions on grocery lists. I have fast and slow versions too. Do you? If I want to be extra fast, I type at my computer. But when I send letters, I slow down and write by hand. I choose a special pen. I reflect. I take my time and make my letter shapes beautiful.

I WONDER HOW LONG THIS PIECE OF SEA GLASS HAS BEEN TOSSED BY THE OCEAN.

• • •

WHY DO TREES HAVE RING PATTERNS INSIDE THEIR TRUNKS?

• • •

HOME-BAKED BREAD IS ESPECIALLY DELICIOUS WHEN STILL WARM.

these things take time

451

Object:

Date: / /

Location: _____

I wonder:

Wild!

452

Date: /   /

Location: _____

☐ Green   ☐ Transparent   ☐ Golden accents

CHRYSALIS

I wonder:

453

Date: /   /

Location: _____

☐ Saltwater taffy   ☐ In action   ☐ Your favorite flavor

TAFFY MACHINE

I wonder:

454

Date: /   /

Location: _____

☐ On roof   ☐ On branch   ☐ Looks dangerous!

ICICLES

I wonder:

455

Date: /   /

Location: _____

☐ Three balls   ☐ Five balls   ☐ More than five

JUGGLING

I wonder:

MEDITATION

Date: / /

Location: _____

☐ Prayer beads ☐ Cushion ☐ Mantra

wonder:

NEEDLEWORK

Date: / /

Location: _____

☐ Tatting ☐ Cross-stitch ☐ Crochet

wonder:

POCKET WATCH

Date: / /

Location: _____

☐ Antique ☐ Wind-up ☐ Broken

wonder:

HAND SAW

Date: / /

Location: _____

☐ Wide-tooth ☐ Fine-tooth ☐ Scent of sawdust

wonder:

460

Date: /   /

SAND TIMER

Location: _____

☐ Made of glass   ☐ In board game   ☐ Watched it run out

I wonder:

461

Date: /   /

SUNDIAL

Location: _____

☐ Handheld   ☐ On sunny day   ☐ On cloudy day

I wonder:

462

Date: /   /

SEA GLASS

Location: _____

☐ Clear   ☐ Green   ☐ Raised letters

I wonder:

463

Date: /   /

HEART-SHAPED STONE

Location: _____

☐ Left where found   ☐ Collected it   ☐ Gifted it away

I wonder:

ERMENTATION

Date: /   /

Location: _____

☐ Sauerkraut   ☐ Kombucha   ☐ Pickles

wonder:

ARKING METER

Date: /   /

Location: _____

☐ Analog   ☐ Digital   ☐ Expired

wonder:

ALL BEING BUILT

Date: /   /

Location: _____

☐ Brick   ☐ Stone   ☐ Snow

wonder:

LOTHES DRYING
N LINE

Date: /   /

Location: _____

☐ Plain   ☐ Colorful   ☐ Underwear

wonder:

468

Date: /   /

Location: _____

DOUGH RISING

☐ First rise   ☐ Final rise   ☐ Punched down by you

I wonder:

469

Date: /   /

Location: _____

INSTANT NOODLES

☐ Spicy   ☐ In a rush   ☐ Seasoning packet

I wonder:

470

Date: /   /

Location: _____

PRACTICING AN INSTRUMENT

☐ Neighbor   ☐ Playing scales   ☐ In your household

I wonder:

471

Date: /   /

Location: _____

RUSTY ITEM

☐ Bucket   ☐ Bicycle chain   ☐ Interesting colors

I wonder:

HANDWRITING

Date: /   /

Location: _____

☐ Cursive   ☐ Letter in the mail   ☐ By someone you love

wonder:

A LOOSE TOOTH

Date: /   /

Location: _____

☐ First one   ☐ Yours   ☐ Swallowed it

wonder:

TREE RINGS

Date: /   /

Location: _____

☐ More than 10   ☐ More than 50   ☐ More than 100

wonder:

A GOOD FRIEND

Date: /   /

Location: _____

☐ Fun   ☐ Good listener   ☐ Many years

wonder:

LASTING LEGACIES

I am surrounded by things that are older than me: my house, my desk, the iron skillet on my stove. Objects—especially well-made, durable ones—stick around. We can enjoy old things because they have life spans much longer than people. This is also true for intangible things, things we can't touch, like stories, folk songs, and dances. We keep them alive by telling them, singing them, and dancing them. We carry them forward and pass them along to future generations.

I am the current caretaker of my great-grandmother Harriet's knitting needle case. It is almost a hundred years old and packed full of needles of all sizes. I need the needles to knit hats and scarves and sweaters, but even more importantly, I need to know *how* to knit. The *how* is not kept inside the case. It is inside me! By far, the best way to learn how to knit is for someone to show you, in person. I fondly recall the summer my grandmother Mary Ann taught me. I was eight. We sat close together on her couch so that we could both get our hands around the needles at the same time. She patiently guided me, again and again, until I could do it on my own.

I WONDER HOW MANY TIMES THIS IRON SKILLET HAS BEEN COOKED IN.

• • •

WHERE AND WHEN WAS THE PRINTING PRESS INVENTED?

• • •

IT IS SURPRISING THAT THIS KNITTING NEEDLE CASE'S ZIPPER HASN'T BROKEN YET.

LASTING LEGACIES

Object:

Date: /   /

Location: _____

I wonder:

477

Date: /   /

Location: _____

NEWSPAPER FROM PREVIOUS CENTURY

☐ Black and white   ☐ In a scrapbook   ☐ The Sunday funnies

I wonder:

478

Date: /   /

Location: _____

OLD DIARY

☐ Ancestor's   ☐ Yours   ☐ Historical figure's

I wonder:

479

Date: /   /

Location: _____

WAX SEAL

☐ Your initial   ☐ In your mailbox   ☐ Love letter

I wonder:

480

Date: /   /

Location: _____

CARD CATALOG

☐ In library   ☐ Cards inside   ☐ At antique fair

I wonder:

DICTIONARY

Date: / /

Location: _____

☐ Finger tabs   ☐ Non-English   ☐ OED

wonder:

HOME MOVIE

Date: / /

Location: _____

☐ VHS tape   ☐ Film reel   ☐ Digital file

wonder:

THRIFT STORE TREASURE

Date: / /

Location: _____

☐ Perfect fit   ☐ A good deal   ☐ Rhinestone glasses

wonder:

FAMILY HEIRLOOM

Date: / /

Location: _____

☐ Textile   ☐ Jewelry   ☐ Kitchenware

wonder:

485 OLD FAMILY RECIPE

Date: / /

Location: _____

☐ Handwritten ☐ Typed ☐ By memory

I wonder:

Candied Orange Peel
Ingredients:
  3 large oranges, cut into strips
  4 cups sugar
  3 cups water
Directions:
  Place peels in large saucepan
  and cover with water. Bring to a

486 FERN

Date: / /

Location: _____

☐ In the forest ☐ Fiddleheads ☐ Moss nearby

I wonder:

487 PHOTO OF YOUR ANCESTOR

Date: / /

Location: _____

☐ Black and white ☐ Color ☐ You know their life story

I wonder:

488 GRAVESTONE

Date: / /

Location: _____

☐ 19th century ☐ Carved designs ☐ Unknown soldier

I wonder:

AN ELECTION

Date: / /

Location: _____

☐ Ballot ☐ Sticker ☐ Sticker in multiple languages

wonder:

FOLK SONG

Date: / /

Location: _____

☐ Live ☐ Recording ☐ Sing-along

wonder:

A GOOD STORY

Date: / /

Location: _____

☐ Book ☐ Told orally ☐ True

wonder:

GOOD TEETH CARE

Date: / /

Location: _____

☐ Mint floss ☐ New toothbrush ☐ Dentist appointment

wonder:

493

Date: /   /

Location: _____

FOSSIL

☐ Ammonite   ☐ Trilobite   ☐ Older than 100 million years

I wonder:

494

Date: /   /

Location: _____

MOLCAJETE

☐ At home   ☐ In restaurant   ☐ Fresh salsa

I wonder:

495

Date: /   /

Location: _____

IRON SKILLET

☐ Well-seasoned   ☐ In the family   ☐ Bought secondhand

I wonder:

496

Date: /   /

Location: _____

A GREAT INVENTION

☐ Wheel   ☐ Printing press   ☐ Vaccine

I wonder:

ANCIENT WRITING

Date: /   /

Location: _____

☐ In clay   ☐ In stone   ☐ On papyrus

wonder:

FAMILY CERAMICS

Date: /   /

Location: _____

☐ In use   ☐ Black-on-white   ☐ Celadon glaze

wonder:

SCIENTIFIC DISCOVERY

Date: /   /

Location: _____

☐ Botany   ☐ Biology   ☐ School project

wonder:

A KIND ACT

Date: /   /

Location: _____

☐ Witnessed   ☐ By you   ☐ Anonymous

wonder:

Did you find **ALL 500 WONDERS?** If so, hooray! If not, hooray! If you had a good adventure, then no matter what, **YOU WIN.** But, don't stop now. This is just the beginning. **WHAT WILL YOU DISCOVER NEXT?**

AUNT LEA *aka* LEA REDMOND

Lea Redmond finds joy as she reveals the extraordinary hiding in the ordinary: a salt shaker, a penny, hand gestures, clouds. Lea lives in Oakland, California, where she creates books, toys, games, and small adventures that invite humans of all ages to be curious, playful, and kind.

Keep in touch with Lea and visit her world of wonder at:
LeaRedmond.com

A few of Lea's favorite things:

 SMALL BASKETS   **BUBBLE GUM MACHINES**

 WHALES   **ANTS**   **BEACH PEBBLES**

 FOUND PENNIES   **GREEN TEA**

 MOTHS  **ANTIQUE STAINED GLASS**   **MAIL**

 DANDELIONS  **URCHIN SHELLS**

Dedicated to:

This book is dedicated to Malcolm and Rhett. We became friends while observing a boxelder bug on the sidewalk together. You are both full of curiosity about the world around you!

Special Thanks:

First and foremost, I thank the myriad wonders scattered abundantly across planet Earth. I regret that I could only feature 500 of you in this book, but I want you to know that each and every one of you is special beyond measure. I promise to keep my eyes open for you. I see you. Thank you for being you. You help me remember who I am, too.

Thank you to my wonderful team at the Collective Book Studio for seeing the promise of this quirky project and working joyfully to offer it to the world. And, especially, I want to thank my editor, Summer Dawn Laurie. You are a wonder! I am dazzled by your intellect, energized by your enthusiasm, inspired by your integrity, and warmed by your heart. It has been a treat to open my eyes wide with you these past months. Next, a hearty thank you to my newsletter subscribers, who submitted hundreds of lists of their favorite wonders, reviewed early drafts of the book, and cheered me on via Patreon. This project has been funded by my generous Kickstarter backers. Thank you for your endless support and enthusiasm over the years!

Library of Congress Cataloging-in-Publication Data available.
ISBN: 978-1-951412-79-1
Library of Congress Control Number: 2021918840

Manufactured in China.
Design by Andrea Kelly.

1 3 5 7 9 10 8 6 4 2

The Collective Book Studio®
Oakland, California
www.thecollectivebook.studio